The
Catechism
Handbook

OTHER WORKS BY OSCAR LUKEFAHR, C.M.

A Catholic Guide to the Bible

The Privilege of Being Catholic

Christ's Mother and Ours

The Search for Happiness

"We Believe…" A Survey of the Catholic Faith

We Worship: A Guide to the Cathoic Mass

We Pray: Living in God's Presence

We Live: To Know, Love, and Serve God

The
Catechism
Handbook

Father Oscar Lukefahr, C. M.

Liguori
ONE LIGUORI DRIVE
LIGUORI MO 63057-9999

Imprimi Potest:
James Shea, C.SS.R.
Provincial, St. Louis Province
The Redemptorists

Imprimatur:
+ Paul Zipfel, V.G.
Auxiliary Bishop, Archdiocese of St. Louis

Library of Congress Cataloging-in-Publication Data
Lukefahr, Oscar.
    The Catechism handbook / Oscar Lukefahr, C.M.
        p. cm.
    Includes index.
    ISBN 978-0-89243-864-8 (pbk.)
    1. Catholic Church. Catechismus Ecclesiae Catolicae. 2. Catholic Church—Catechism. I. Title.
BX1959.5.L85 1996
238'.2—dc20   95-45290

Liguori Publications, a nonprofit corporation, is an apostolate of the Redemptorists. To learn more about the Redemptorists, visit Redemptorists.com.

Copyright © 1996, Oscar Lukefahr, C.M.
Printed in the United States of America
11   14 13

To order, call 800-325-9521
www.liguori.org

<u>DEDICATION</u>

*To the friends who, through the years,
have brought God's love into my life*

CONTENTS

FOREWORD ix

INTRODUCTION xi

CHAPTER ONE: Ancient Truths for Modern Times 1

PART ONE: The Profession of Faith

CHAPTER TWO: Why Are We Here? 9

CHAPTER THREE: Belief in God 15

CHAPTER FOUR: Jesus Christ 23

CHAPTER FIVE: The Holy Spirit and the Church 31

CHAPTER SIX: Life Here and Life Everlasting 39

PART TWO: The Celebration of the Christian Mystery

CHAPTER SEVEN: Liturgy and the Sacraments of Initiation 49

CHAPTER EIGHT: Sacraments of Healing and Service 61

PART THREE: Life in Christ

CHAPTER NINE: Life in Christ 71

CHAPTER TEN: Law, Grace, Commandments, and Love of God 79

CHAPTER ELEVEN: God's Commandments and Love of Neighbor 87

PART FOUR: Christian Prayer

CHAPTER TWELVE: Prayer 97

EPILOGUE 105

INDEX 107

ABOUT THE AUTHOR 111

FOREWORD

I was privileged to be at the Vatican ceremony in which Pope John Paul II officially gave the world the new *Catechism of the Catholic Church*. It had been 426 years since a similar catechism, the *Roman Catechism*, had been published by the Church. Fortunate are we who live at the time when such a summary of Catholic belief and practice becomes available.

To his previous books about things Catholic, Father Oscar Lukefahr, C.M., now adds *The Catechism Handbook*. He does so "to promote interest and enthusiasm for the *Catechism of the Catholic Church*." I believe and pray that his stated purpose will be realized.

The Catechism Handbook is not a substitute for the new *Catechism* itself. Father Lukefahr wisely advises that when a person obtains a copy of the *Catechism*, the first thing to do is familiarize oneself with it. Look it over. Examine the Contents to see how the *Catechism* is organized. Page through its Subject Index. Search cross references in margins of its pages for additional information about a particular topic.

Although many others could use *The Catechism Handbook* to their personal profit, it is especially for Catholics. If the *Catechism of the Catholic Church* is a summary of Catholic teaching, *The Catechism Handbook* is a summary of the summary—a "reader's digest" that leads one to the original and complete text. The new *Catechism* itself recognizes the value of such an approach through its "In Brief" sections at the end of each thematic unit.

Like the *Catechism* itself, *The Catechism Handbook* can be used to advantage by all Catholics—those who want to know more accurately and fully their Church's teaching and those (I say this with charity) who don't know they don't know their Church's teaching because, erroneously, they think they already know. (See page 2: "But Is It Really Needed?")

Of the *Catechism of the Catholic Church*, Pope John Paul II said, "I declare it to be a sure norm for teaching the faith." With its convenient style, *The Catechism Handbook* can present that "sure norm" to many people.

MOST REVEREND JOHN J. LEIBRECHT
BISHOP OF SPRINGFIELD-CAPE GIRARDEAU
AUGUST 1995

INTRODUCTION

The purpose of this handbook is to promote interest and enthusiasm for the *Catechism of the Catholic Church* and to guide readers through the *Catechism*. The *Catechism* is a wonderful resource, but its length and language can be intimidating to those who want to read it cover to cover or use it as a reference.

This handbook aims at being "user-friendly" and at making the *Catechism* more user-friendly. It summarizes the content of the *Catechism* in an easy-to-read style, explains difficult issues, and draws attention to areas of special importance. At the end of each chapter, it presents questions for discussion or reflection as well as activities to help readers apply the truths of the *Catechism* to their own lives.

People who wish to read the entire *Catechism* can utilize this handbook to preview and review each section. Getting a "bird's eye view" of a lengthy section will help readers grasp its content in advance. Rereading the handbook after studying the *Catechism* can help readers retain what they have covered.

Those who intend to use the *Catechism* primarily as a reference can get a good idea of the entire *Catechism* from this handbook. By providing the context for any selected passage, the handbook makes it more understandable.

This handbook and its accompanying workbook will be useful for personal or group study, adult religious education classes, RCIA programs, high school religious education classes, and other applications where time limits or other considerations might make study of the whole *Catechism* impractical.

Readers are encouraged to obtain a copy of the *Catechism*. Based on the documents of the Second Vatican Council and approved by our Holy Father, it sets forth the teachings of the Church for all believers. As Catholics throughout the world become more familiar with the *Catechism* and with the doctrine that has been handed down from the apostles, we will, more and more, "come to the unity of the faith and of the knowledge of the Son of God" (Ephesians 4:13).

FATHER OSCAR LUKEFAHR, C.M.

P.S. Sincere thanks to all who helped in the development of this book. To Father Allan Weinert, C.SS.R., who approved the series of *Liguorian* articles on which this book was based, and to Cheryl Plass, who did a great job of editing those articles. To Barbara McElroy, for her patience and expertise in editing this book and its accompanying workbook. To Cecelia Portlock, for her attention to the details of production. To Kass Dotterweich, for her editorial assistance. To Grady Gunter, for his talent and attention to the cover and interior design. To Joan Ruhl, who proofread the manuscript and workbook. To those who helped at various stages of the project: Father Anthony Falanga, C.M., Rob and Sallie Hurley, Henry and Jeanne Moreno, Father Arthur Trapp, C.M., Den and Kathy Vollink, Brock and Kathy Whittenberger. To Meghan, Mary Beth, Stephanie, and Chip, and all the children who bring laughter and love. To the members of adult religion classes at Saint Vincent de Paul Parish in Perryville, Missouri, who once again helped keep me on schedule and provided ideas and moral support. To my sister, Joann Lukefahr, D.C., who made arrangements for the class. To Bishop John Leibrecht, who wrote the Foreword and provided a great deal of encouragement. May God bless you all!

Chapter One

ANCIENT TRUTHS
FOR MODERN TIMES

"Our lives are short," said Rob, "and we see things from the perspective of the few years we're here on earth. The Church has been guided by the Holy Spirit for two thousand years, and it teaches what millions of people have learned from Jesus Christ, the Son of God. I would be foolish if I didn't pay attention to what the Church offers."

Rob was treasurer and chief financial officer of a National Football League team for eighteen years. He was around the glamour of professional sports long enough to realize that fame and fortune do not guarantee happiness or peace of mind. Professional football may provide excitement and diversion, but it doesn't answer the most basic questions in life: Why are we here? Where are we going? How should we live? For the answers to these questions, for the wisdom and direction we all need to find meaning, Rob looks to the Church.

Rob and others like him now have a great resource to help them, the *Catechism of the Catholic Church*. Rob and I discussed the *Catechism* shortly after its publication in English on June 22, 1994. His remarks about the importance of Church teaching shed light on one of the primary values of the *Catechism*. It takes the wisdom distilled from twenty centuries of humanity's quest for God and places it in our hands.

A "One Volume Library"

The *Catechism of the Catholic Church* gathers Church teaching from many sources into one convenient, readable volume. In a certain sense, it is the "Catechism of the Second Vatican Council." It arranges the teachings of the Council in logical order for study and reflection. It integrates them with the great sources of belief, such as the Bible, the liturgy, instructions of previous Church councils and popes, and the works of prominent teachers like Augustine, Thomas Aquinas, and Teresa of Avila.

Before the *Catechism* was available, students of Catholicism might have had to look through Second Vatican Council documents for answers to one question and through *The Code of Canon Law* for answers to another. They might have had to consult a Catholic encyclopedia for information about devotion to Mary, and search libraries and Catholic bookstores to discover what the Church teaches about issues that have arisen since Vatican II, like in vitro fertilization. Most Catholics have had neither the resources nor the theological background necessary for such tasks. Now they can find what the Church teaches about most issues simply by turning to the *Catechism of the Catholic Church*.

"But Is It Really Needed?"

Not long ago I attended a banquet to honor an active Catholic leader, and was seated with Catholics from several different parishes. A conversation started about religious education programs. Julie said the teacher in her son's third-grade religion class told the children that praying the rosary was no longer recommended. Her tenth-grader's parish youth director taught that only baptized Christians would go to heaven. Norma said her daughter's high school religious education teacher, who converted to Catholicism from a fundamentalist church three years ago, stated that Mary and Joseph had other children after Jesus. Kathy, who had volunteered to serve as a teacher in a parish program for parents preparing to have children baptized, added that she was told by her parish director of religious education not to mention original sin to the parents because it was not really relevant to infant Baptism.

As director of a Catholic home-study program, I often hear similar statements. Parish catechists face real challenges. Busy individuals—who may be raising a family, holding down a job, and serving several civic organizations—are asked by their pastor to teach in a parish religion program. Because they want to help, they make heroic sacrifices and do their best, but they may have few opportunities to get the kind of education in Scripture and theology they need to answer the many questions posed to them. When asked about Church teaching on this or that issue, they haven't had an adequate resource to help them find the answers—until now.

Each of the concerns voiced at the banquet, for example, is discussed in the *Catechism of the Catholic Church*. The *Catechism* recommends the rosary as a form of prayerful reflection that is of great value (C 971, 2678, 2708). (References to the *Catechism* will be given as "C" followed by paragraph numbers.) It explains that those who are ignorant of the Gospel but seek the truth and do God's will, in accordance with their understanding of it, can be saved (C 1260). It relates why the Church has always taught that the "brothers and sisters" of Jesus were not children of Mary, but relatives and followers of Christ (C 499-507). The *Catechism* mentions original sin in declaring the importance of infant Baptism (C 1250) and explains it as an essential truth of Catholicism (C 388-409).

If parish religious education teachers need solid information on the faith, we can be sure that most other Catholics do too! The *Catechism of the Catholic Church* is now available to provide that information in a convenient, readable, and inexpensive format. When questions are raised at a child's religion class or an adult study group, the *Catechism* can provide answers. If you are asked to be a godparent at a child's Baptism, you can review the Church's teaching about this sacrament in the *Catechism*. If a debate starts at work about euthanasia, assisted suicide, and discontinuing medical procedures, you can read in the *Catechism* how the Church applies the fifth commandment to each of these issues. If you'd like advice on different forms of prayer, you will find it in the *Catechism*.

What the *Catechism* Is, and Isn't

"I was surprised to see that the *Catechism* isn't in question-and-answer form," remarked Tony. "I was pleasantly surprised to find that it's quite readable." The essence of a catechism is not the question-answer format, but its teaching function. *Catechism* comes from the Greek word *catechein*, which means "to teach," and in the early Church, those to whom the faith was being taught were called *catechumens*. In the sixteenth century the word *catechism* was coined to refer to a book or manual used to teach religious doctrine.

While many manuals for instructing people in religion have been created over the centuries, the first official Catholic catechism for the whole Church was commissioned by the Council of Trent. It was completed in 1566 and was called the *Roman Catechism*. (The old *Baltimore Catechism* was a simplified English version of the *Roman Catechism* in question-and-answer form). The *Catechism of the Catholic Church* is the successor to the *Roman Catechism*.

The *Catechism* is not a revision of the basic teachings of the Church. The Catholic Church believes that the "deposit of faith," the fundamental truths necessary for salvation (eternal happiness with God in heaven) and found in the Bible and sacred Tradition of the Church, cannot be changed or added to. But the Church can grow in its understanding of these basic truths and can improve the clarity with which it expresses them. The Church must constantly apply its teachings to ever-changing situations. The *Catechism of the Catholic Church* expresses ancient truths in modern language and applies basic principles to today's issues, problems like organ transplants, artificial insemination, and the limits of medical research.

The *Catechism* is intended as an official statement of the Catholic faith, and is directed primarily to bishops, priests, catechists, and publishers of local catechisms. It is not designed as a religion text for children, but it should be the doctrinal foundation for future textbooks. It can be used as a classroom reference book; a teacher, for example, might assign a topic, such as a particular sacrament, for students to look up and report on. It is appropriate reading for anyone, young or old, who wishes to know what the Church teaches.

Using the *Catechism*

The *Catechism* may be read "cover to cover." This is no small task, since there are almost seven hundred pages of text, but it is certainly possible. Some people have told me that they've enjoyed reading the *Catechism*. They had expected something like a telephone directory or computer manual. Instead, they found language that is clear, intelligible, and sometimes quite moving. Doctrinal passages, for example, are interspersed with quotations from Scripture, the liturgy, great teachers of the past, poets, and saints. Reading the entire *Catechism* requires diligence and persistence, but its subject matter and fine quality will provide ample rewards to all who do so. If you cover just two pages a day, you will read the entire *Catechism* in less than a year!

The *Catechism* may also be used as a reference work, like an encyclopedia or medical dictionary. It is well designed for this purpose. It offers a detailed outline in the Contents. There are more than one hundred pages of indexes, including those of Scripture quotes, Church councils, papal teachings, various ecclesiastical documents, and writers, plus an extensive Subject Index that provides quick access to every significant topic in the *Catechism*. Other features which make the *Catechism* more useful include cross-referencing of related subjects and a paragraph-numbering structure allowing quick access to specific topics. A second edition published in 2000 made minor changes in the text and added a glossary at the end.

The *Catechism* can be obtained at Liguori Publications (1-800-325-9521) or at bookstores, Catholic religious-supply shops, and even at some discount stores. Since its publication the *Catechism* has been selling briskly, and it is finding an honored place next to the Bible in many Catholic homes.

Reading the Instructions

"When all else fails, read the instructions." Better yet, read them first to keep all else from failing! Those who study the *Catechism of the Catholic Church* should "read the instructions." They are found in Pope John Paul II's Apostolic Constitution "The Deposit of Faith," which opens the *Catechism*, and in the Prologue (C 1-25).

A Word From Pope John Paul II

John Paul II noted that the principal task given to the Second Vatican Council (1962-1965) by Pope John XXIII was to make Christian doctrine more accessible to all. The Council produced many documents explaining the content of our faith. Twenty years after Vatican II ended, an assembly of bishops at Rome requested of Pope John Paul that a catechism be composed to make the Council's teaching more available. The pope set in motion a worldwide effort to involve bishops, theologians, and catechists in writing a catechism. In 1992 it was published as the *Catechism of the Catholic Church*, "a sure norm for teaching the faith."

Pope John Paul stated four purposes for the *Catechism*. First, it is intended for Church leaders as an "authentic reference text for teaching catholic doctrine and particularly for preparing local catechisms." Second, it is offered to all the faithful who wish to deepen their knowledge of the Church's teachings. Third, it is meant to promote ecumenical dialogue because it shows the content and harmony of our faith. Fourth, it is for all who want to know what the Catholic Church believes.

Prologue to the *Catechism*

The Prologue opens by answering life's most pressing question: "Why are we here?" We are here to know and love God. God sent Jesus to proclaim this and gather us into the unity of God's family. Jesus in turn sent his apostles to preach. All who welcome their message and follow Christ are called to spread his teaching throughout the world (C 1-3).

The process by which the Good News of Jesus is handed on is called catechesis. Periods of renewal in the Church, such as the era after the Council of Trent, have been special times of catechesis. In the years following Vatican II, catechesis has been emphasized and has found concrete expression in the *Catechism of the Catholic Church* (C 4-10).

The aim of the *Catechism* is to present a synthesis of the essential contents of Catholic doctrine—faith and morals—in the light of the Second Vatican Council and the whole of the Church's Tradition. The *Catechism* is divided into four main parts: The Profession of Faith, belief; The Celebration of the Christian Mystery, worship; Life in Christ, Christian life; and Christian Prayer (C 11-17).

At this point, a careful examination of the Contents and the Subject Index can help us see the *Catechism* as a unified whole. An Index of Abbreviations of Church documents and books of the Bible is found after the Subject Index; these abbreviations are used in footnotes throughout the *Catechism*. Preceding the Subject Index there is an extensive Index of Citations showing where readers may find quotations from the Bible, Church documents, and Catholic authors. If, for example, we would like to know how the *Catechism* interprets Matthew 16:18, "You are Peter, and on this rock I will build my church," we locate Matthew 16:18 in the Index of Citations. There we find numbers 424, 442, 552, 586, and 869 directing us to paragraphs in the *Catechism* explaining Matthew 16:18. We may also use the Index of Citations to become more familiar with Church documents or to find where certain authors, like Teresa of Avila or Thomas More, are quoted.

Cross references, italicized numbers in the margins, call our attention to paragraphs that deal with similar themes. Small print is used throughout the *Catechism* for quotations and supplementary explanations. Each unit concludes with an "In Brief" summary (C 18-22).

The Prologue closes by explaining that catechetical methods used to present the *Catechism* must be adapted to the needs of those to whom it is addressed. Doctrine should be presented in such a way that the love of Christ shines through (C 23-25).

Members of the Church, Guided by the Spirit

Our lives are short, and our hearts are restless with questions about God and the purpose of human existence. Jesus Christ entered the world two thousand years ago as God's perfect answer to our questions. For twenty centuries the Church, under the guidance of the Holy Spirit, has reflected on Christ's life and teaching. The *Catechism of the Catholic Church* is the handbook offered us by all the believers who have gone before. If we accept and use it, it will help us discover the answers to our questions. It will direct us to the One our hearts seek and to the happiness we long for.

Questions for Discussion or Reflection

What kind of religious education did you have? Could you have benefited from the *Catechism of the Catholic Church* had it been available? What questions do you have about the Church's teaching that might be answered in the *Catechism*? What do you think are the most basic questions in life?

Activities

Skim through the *Catechism,* and become familiar with its contents. Do the exercises suggested in the section "Prologue to the *Catechism*." Ask the Holy Spirit to open your mind and heart to the truths of our faith expressed in the *Catechism*.

Part One

The
Profession
of Faith

Chapter Two

WHY ARE WE HERE?

Stephanie, age six, told her parents, Ed and Cathy, that she was studying about God in first grade at her Catholic school. "It's really hard," she said, "to understand how God can see everything and be everywhere." Ed started to explain the need for faith, but Chip, Stephanie's younger brother, interrupted: "That's nothing. What I can't understand is how the Easter bunny gets those baskets around to all the houses!"

The desire for God is imprinted in our hearts. We seek God from childhood through old age. At times we feel very close to God; at other times we wonder if God, like the Easter bunny, might be just a figment of our imaginations. But Easter eggs can be explained without the bunny. The universe cannot be explained without God. Neither can the longings of our hearts. The world and we who live on it had a beginning we cannot account for. We strive for a happiness that is beyond us. Our origin and our final end can be found only in God (C 26-35).

Supernatural Revelation

While it is possible to know that God exists by reason alone, God has not left us to our own resources in seeking knowledge about our Creator and the origin and purpose of our lives. Rather, God has revealed truth in ways "above nature," in supernatural Revelation (C 36-38).

When we study Revelation, language falls short. But created things bear a certain resemblance to God, so we can speak of God by taking creatures as a starting point. We can look at the beauty of a sunset, for example, and say that God's beauty goes far beyond that. But we must always realize that our language will never exhaust the mystery of God (C 39-49).

God, aware of our limitations, has communicated information to us gradually, in stages. The first revelation made to Adam and Eve was that God existed. When they sinned, God offered forgiveness and salvation. God's covenant (agreement) with Noah expressed the reality that people tended to worship God as groups or nations. Unfortunately, this often resulted in paganism and idolatry (C 50-58).

So God called a man, Abram, who responded in faith. Renamed Abraham, he founded a family which would become God's Chosen People (known as Israel or the Jewish nation). When descendants of Abraham were enslaved in Egypt, God called Moses to lead them to freedom. God made a covenant with them and gave them the Ten Commandments to guide them. Through centuries of ups and downs, holy men and women nurtured Israel's faith, declaring that God would bring redemption. These people preceded Jesus Christ, God's Son and Word of salvation. In Jesus, God brought public Revelation to completion, though Christians will only gradually grasp its full significance. All private revelations and visions are subordinate to God's Revelation in Christ. They cannot improve it, but can help us live it more fully (C 59-73).

Divine Revelation: Tradition and Scripture

Christ commanded his apostles to bring his Gospel to the world. They did so in two ways, *orally* through their preaching and *in writing* through the Scriptures. The apostles left bishops as their successors in handing on Christ's teaching, and the unbroken transmission of Revelation by the Church under the guidance of the Holy Spirit is called Tradition (C 74-79).

From one divine source, therefore, Revelation is passed down in two distinct ways, namely, Scripture and Tradition. Both are directed by the Holy Spirit and both are to be equally reverenced. Tradition comes from the apostles and passes on what they learned from Jesus and the Holy Spirit. It should be distinguished from local traditions and customs which develop over time and which are subject to change (C 80-83).

Deposit of Faith and Its Interpretation

The content of Tradition and Scripture is called the "deposit of faith." Authentic interpretation of this deposit is the task of the bishops in union with the pope (the *magisterium*). Essential truths are proclaimed as dogmas, which mark our way along the path of faith and are to be believed by all Catholics. The faithful share in understanding and handing on these dogmas and other revealed truths. Moreover, the Church teaches that the whole body of the faithful cannot err in matters of belief when together with the bishops they manifest a universal consent in matters of faith and morals. As believers study and preach the deposit of faith, they grow in their understanding of what God has revealed (C 84-100).

Sacred Scripture

God speaks to us in human words through sacred Scripture, and so God is the author of the Scriptures. Scripture was written by human beings who used their own abilities under God's inspiration, and they are also true authors (C 101-106).

Because God is author, "we must acknowledge that the books of Scripture firmly, faithfully, and without error teach that truth which God, for the sake of our salvation, wished to see confided to the Sacred Scriptures" (*Dei Verbum 11* cited in C 107). Because human beings are authors, we must be attentive to their intentions in writing, to conditions of time and culture, to literary styles, and to ways of speaking and writing. Christianity is a religion not of the book, but of the Word, Jesus Christ. Jesus must open our minds to the meaning of Scripture, and the Bible must be interpreted with the help of the Holy Spirit. Since the Bible was given by God to the Church, the Bible is authentically interpreted within the Church. The Church offers three principles of special importance in such interpretation. First, we must be attentive to the content and unity of the whole Bible. Second, we must read the Bible within the living Tradition of the Church. Third, we must be attentive to the "analogy of faith," the coherence of truths among themselves (C 107-114).

The Church distinguishes various senses in which Scripture may be interpreted. The *literal* sense is the meaning intended by the author. The *spiritual* sense depends on the literal, but sees it as a sign pointing to a deeper meaning. This may be *allegorical*, where one event foreshadows another (crossing the Red Sea is a foreshadowing of Baptism). It may be *moral*, leading us to act justly. It may be *anagogical*, meaning that earthly realities point to our heavenly goal (C 115-119).

The Books of the Bible

The Catholic Church accepts forty-six Old Testament and twenty-seven New Testament books in the canon (official list) of the Bible. The Old Testament is imperfect and provisional, but it points to Christ. The New Testament focuses on the teaching and life of Christ and on the Church he founded (C 120-124).

The Gospels are the heart of Scripture. They developed in three stages. The first was the life and teaching of Jesus. The second was the oral preaching of the early followers of Jesus. The third was the writing of the Gospels, as the evangelists collected materials about Jesus and adapted them to meet the needs of specific groups (C 125-127).

The Old and New Testaments are closely interrelated. The Old prefigures the New, and the New must be read in the light of the Old. The Church urges all the faithful to study the Bible and emphasizes the Bible's importance for theology, catechetics, and preaching. As Saint Jerome said, "Ignorance of the Scriptures is ignorance of Christ" (C 128-141).

Our Response to God: Faith

Through Revelation, God addresses us as friends and invites us to intimate union. The proper response to God is faith, by which we submit intellect and will to God in the obedience of faith. Abraham is a model of faith in the Old Testament. In the New Testament, Mary perfectly embodies the obedience of faith (C 142-149).

By faith, we unite ourselves to God and we give our assent to the whole truth God has revealed. To believe in God is also to believe in Jesus Christ and in the Holy Spirit. Jesus reveals God to us and the Holy Spirit enables us to believe (C 150-152).

Faith is a grace, a gift from God, a supernatural virtue infused by God. It is also a human act, by which we freely put our trust in God and believe what God has revealed. We do not understand everything God reveals, but faith is reasonable because the miracles of Christ and the growth of the Church show God's hand at work (C 153-156).

Faith is certain because it is based on God's word. Faith seeks to know God and to understand God's word better. While faith is above reason, it does not contradict reason or truths gained from science; truth cannot contradict truth (C 157-159).

Faith must be free. God does not force us to believe even though faith is necessary for salvation. Faith can be lost through neglect and sin, and we must nurture faith by study, prayer, and works of charity. When the trials of this imperfect world shake our faith, we should turn to model believers like Abraham and Mary. Above all, we must look to Jesus, the "pioneer and perfecter of our faith" (Hebrews 12:2; C 160-165).

Faith is a personal act, but we receive faith from others and should hand it on. The faith of the Church is professed personally by each believer ("I believe") and by the liturgical assembly of believers ("We believe"). The Church is our mother, our teacher in the faith. The Church guards the faith and gives us formulas, the Creeds, by which we profess our faith and remain one in the faith. "Through the centuries, in so many languages, cultures, peoples, and nations, the Church has constantly confessed this one faith, received from the one Lord, transmitted by the one Baptism, and grounded in the conviction that all people have only one God and Father" (C 166-184).

Like Stephanie, we can't understand God, but we can believe. And so we move on to study the meaning of faith.

Questions for Discussion or Reflection

What do you think are the most important reasons for believing in God? What are the main causes of doubt about the existence of God? When have you felt most certain about the reality of God? When have you been most tested by doubt?

Activities

After reading the section, "Our Response to God: Faith," quietly reflect on your relationship to God and on the place God has had in your life up to this time. In your own words, speak to God about faith, and ask God to strengthen your faith.

Chapter Three

BELIEF IN GOD

"Several years ago I felt almost desperate to have faith. I'll never forget going to the Catholic pastor, scared to death. I asked him how a person gets faith. I had heard it was a gift. Perhaps a gift I wasn't given? 'Pray for faith,' he said. I did. It was a first step, one which led me into the Catholic Church. God gives grace to believe, and we must pray for it. I still do."

This testimony of a recent convert reminds us that faith is God-centered. Faith is obedient assent to what God has revealed. God, by grace, enables us to believe. God gives us the Church to clarify what we profess in its creeds.

The Creeds

From New Testament times, Christians have expressed their beliefs in formulas called professions of faith or creeds—from the Latin, *credo*, "I believe" (C 185-188).

Professions of faith are first made when we are baptized in the name of the Father, Son, and Holy Spirit. Creeds are accordingly divided into three parts: the Father and creation, the Son and redemption, the Holy Spirit and sanctification (C 189-190).

Of the many creeds written by church communities, councils, and popes, two are of special importance. The *Apostles' Creed* is a summary of the apostles' faith; it is the Creed of the Roman Church. The *Niceno-Constantinopolitan*, or *Nicene* Creed, comes from the first two ecumenical councils of the Church, held at Nicaea (A.D. 325) and Constantinople (A.D. 381). The *Catechism* follows the Apostles' Creed in its presentation of the faith, supplementing it with references to the Nicene Creed. Ancient tradition lists twelve major articles of the Creed. The *Catechism* names these articles in the Contents and organizes its explanation of the Creed around them (C 191-197).

"I believe in God"

Our profession of faith begins with God, for everything in the universe comes from God and is related to God. We believe in *one* God because there can be only one supreme being. But the one God is, as Jesus revealed, a Trinity of Persons: Father, Son, and Holy Spirit (C 198-202).

A name tells who a person is and allows us to relate to that person. God, when asked for a name by Moses, said "YHWH" (YAHWEH), meaning, "I AM WHO AM." God always *is*. God is a *Being* who depends on no one else. God's mysterious presence and power are such that the Israelites would not even pronounce God's name. Instead, they substituted the title "Lord." Recognizing God's graciousness and mercy, they proclaimed that God always *is*, while material things pass away (C 203-213).

God always *is* the same. Therefore, God is truth, for God never says one thing while meaning another. God is revealed in wisdom, above all in God's Word, Jesus Christ (C 214-217).

God always *is* love, an eternal exchange of love among Father, Son, and Holy Spirit. Their everlasting love is extended to us (C 218-221).

Believing in God means coming to know God's greatness and living in thanksgiving. It means recognizing the dignity of all who are formed in God's image, making good use of created things, and trusting God in every circumstance (C 222-231).

The Trinity

We are baptized in the name of the Father, Son, and Holy Spirit. Our lives and our faith originate in God, who is a Trinity of Persons. That there are three persons in one God is a mystery we cannot fully understand, but God has revealed it as the foundational truth of our faith. All other truths spring from this essential mystery. Theology, the study of God, centers on God as Trinity, and God is revealed to us in the "economy" of salvation, the works by which God creates, redeems, and sanctifies us (C 232-237).

God is addressed as "Father" in the Old Testament. This implies that God is the origin of everything and cares for us as children. Jesus revealed that God is Father in a deeper sense through relationship to him, the Son. The New Testament states that the Son, the Word, is God. The Council of Nicaea taught that the Son is consubstantial with, that is, one with the Father (C 238-242).

Jesus promised to send an Advocate, the Holy Spirit. He thus revealed the Holy Spirit as the third divine Person. Just as the Father sent Jesus to redeem us, so the Father and the Son sent the Holy Spirit to sanctify us. The Spirit is equal to the Father and the Son and proceeds from them both (C 243-248).

That God is Father, Son, and Holy Spirit, yet one God, is the central mystery of our faith. Formulations stating the Christian belief in the Trinity abound in the New Testament. In addition, the Church has expressed its belief in the Trinity with the help of philosophical terminology. We acknowledge one divine nature (substance, essence) and three divine Persons. The Trinity is one, but the divine Persons are really distinct from one another in the way they relate to one another as Father, Son, and Holy Spirit (C 249-256).

Whatever God does proceeds from the Father, Son, and Holy Spirit as one principle of operation. But God's works are done according to the unique personal properties of Father, Son, and Spirit: from the Father, through the Son, in the Holy Spirit. The Trinity is made known to us especially through creation and the missions (sending) of the Son and the Holy Spirit. These missions call each of us to union with God, to be a dwelling place for the Trinity (C 257-267).

"The Father almighty"

God is almighty because God can do all things. God's power is expressed in loving care, in adopting us as children, and in granting infinite mercy to us. God's power is mysterious, especially in its approach to evil. At times God seems incapable of stopping evil, as when Christ suffered death on the cross. Nevertheless, we are challenged to believe, as Mary did, that nothing is impossible with God, that God will conquer evil and bring life from death (C 268-278).

"Creator of heaven and earth"

We believe that God made all things. In this fact we find the answer to life's most basic questions: Where do we come from and where are we going? Scientific studies of the development of life forms and of the appearance of human beings on earth can be helpful in explaining the *when* and *how* of creation. But religion must study the *why* of creation, its meaning and purpose. Christianity, in its explanation of the meaning of creation, follows God's Revelation—especially the first three chapters of Genesis—as well as principles of sound reasoning (C 279-289).

Christianity proclaims that God created from nothing everything that exists. The New Testament further reveals that creation is the work of the Trinity. The Father created all things through the Word and in the Holy Spirit (C 290-292).

The world was made to communicate the glory of God to created beings. God wants us to share in divine life and love and thereby find perfect happiness. The world is not an accident, the result of blind chance. It comes from the wisdom and love of God. It is good, for it originates in the goodness of God. Even though God is greater than created things, God is present to us and holds us in existence. Everything in the universe depends upon God at every moment (C 293-301).

Divine Providence

Creation is good, but not perfect. God created it in a condition of incompletion or process, in a state of journeying toward an ultimate perfection. The way God watches over and guides the universe toward its goal is called *divine providence*. God cares for, as Jesus teaches, even the smallest parts of creation (C 302-305).

In God's plan, we are called to cooperate intelligently and freely with God and thus complete the work of creation. God, the first cause, operates through us as secondary causes. God invites us to enter into the divine plan by our actions, our prayer, and even our suffering (C 306-308).

The Problem of Evil

If God created the world good, if God cares for us, then why do evil and suffering exist? There is no easy answer, and every aspect of the Christian faith fits into the ultimate solution. In particular, the two facts mentioned above—that the world exists in a state of incompletion and that we are called to cooperate freely with God—help us confront the problem of evil (C 309).

Because the world is in process, some beings have to disappear to make room for others. Some things must be torn down so that others may be built up. In a limited world, physical good necessarily involves *physical evil* (C 310).

Because we are called to cooperate freely, we are able to refuse and oppose God's plan. When human beings disobey God, they sin, and *moral evil* enters the world. God does not desire moral evil, but permits it so that we may be free. Further, God can defeat evil by bringing good from it. This is most clearly seen in the death and Resurrection of Jesus (C 311-312).

Why did God not create a world where everything would be complete and all would be forced to do God's will? This sounds attractive. But would we be happy in a world where we could do nothing to make it better? Would we be able to love if we were unable to choose freely? Human life as we know it has meaning only if we can contribute. We can love only if we are free to choose. We perceive only a small part of God's plan in our few years on earth. In eternity, the ways of God's providence will finally be made known (C 313-324).

Heaven and Earth

By heaven and earth, the Creed means everything that exists. Heaven refers to the angels, personal and immortal spiritual beings who are created by God and possess intelligence and free will. The word *angel* means "messenger," and angels are mentioned throughout Scripture as those who do God's will and care for people. Angels adore and minister to Christ. Angels watch over and protect us as members of the Church, and we enjoy their company on life's journey (C 325-336).

God created the earth—the visible, material world. The Book of Genesis symbolically presents creation as a succession of six days of divine work to teach us basic truths about the created order. All things owe their existence to God. Every creature is good, and we must respect this goodness, avoiding any disordered use of things which would show disrespect for the Creator and harm people and the environment. Creatures are interdependent and need one another. The beauty of the universe comes from the diversity of created beings and the relationships among them. There is a hierarchy of creatures, and while all are important, humanity is the summit of the Creator's work. There is a solidarity among creatures because all are created by God and ordered to God's glory. That glory is expressed in the Sabbath rest, which reminds us that we must orient ourselves to God, especially in worship. For Christians, this is the day of the Lord's Resurrection, which signals a new creation where all things find meaning and purpose in Christ (C 337-354).

Humanity

We human beings occupy a unique place in the universe because we are made in the image and likeness of God. We are capable of knowing and loving our Creator. We are one because of a common origin and because of our unity in Christ (C 355-361).

The Bible says, in symbolic language, that God formed us from the ground and breathed life into us. We are soul and body, soul referring to the spiritual principle in us and body referring to our material being. Together, soul and body form a unity, our human nature. The soul is created directly by God, not by parents. It is immortal and will be reunited with the body at the Final Resurrection (C 362-368).

God made human beings male and female. In God's image, man and woman have equal dignity, but they reflect God's perfections in different ways. They are meant to form a communion of persons and to transmit human life, thus sharing in the Creator's work (C 369-373).

God created the first human beings in a state of holiness and original justice. In

God's design, human beings were intended to live free of suffering and death, in harmony with self, others, and creation (C 374-384).

Sin

This design was interrupted by sin, humanity's rejection of God. While the story of the Fall in Genesis 3 is told in figurative language, it relates a real event, an original fault committed by our first parents at the beginning of human history (C 385-390).

Our first parents were tempted by a fallen angel, called Satan or the devil. Satan and other evil spirits were created good by God, but they irrevocably rejected God, becoming evil by their own choice. They are permitted by God to continue in existence, and while the evil they do can cause great harm, they cannot defeat God or destroy the kingdom of Christ (C 391-395).

Original Sin

Genesis says that God told the first humans not to eat of the tree of the knowledge of good and evil. This symbolically expresses that we must accept God's laws which tell us what is good and what is evil. But the first human beings disobeyed God's command. Seduced by the devil, they preferred themselves to God, thinking they could thereby be like God (C 396-398).

Instead, their sin brought tragic consequences. Satan gave them a false image of God as one who was jealous to keep power from them. They became afraid of God. They lost the soul's control over the body, the accord between man and woman, harmony with creation, and freedom from death (C 399-400).

Sin flooded the world and has affected all of history. It has affected us, for we are drawn toward what is wrong and trapped by evils which cannot come from God. This can be understood only in connection with the sin of our first parents (C 401-403).

Because of their sin, our first parents transmitted a human nature deprived of holiness and justice, a state known as original sin. Original sin does not wholly corrupt human nature. But it does deprive us of original holiness and weakens our natural powers. It subjects us to ignorance, suffering, and death. It gives us an inclination toward sin called *concupiscence*. As a result, we must struggle with sin. We are tempted by Satan and negatively influenced by sinful situations in society (C 404-409).

God never abandoned sinful humanity. God promised our first parents that the serpent would be defeated by a descendant of the woman. Christianity sees this to have been accomplished in the person of the new Adam, Jesus Christ, who brings salvation—the restoration of God's life and love, here and forever. It sees a new Eve in Mary, the mother of Christ, who was uniquely victorious over sin, in that God's grace preserved her from original sin and kept her free of all personal sin (C 410-421).

"We believe in God." Each time we recite the Creed and profess what we believe, we can also ask for the grace of a stronger faith. "God gives grace to believe, and we must pray for it!"

Questions for Discussion or Reflection

God created the universe. Have you any idea about the size of the universe or of its magnificence? How many stars are there in our Milky Way galaxy? How many galaxies are there? What do these facts tell us about the greatness of God?

How have you experienced God's providence in your life?

What do you think of the *Catechism's* explanation of evil? Could we be happy if we could do nothing to make the world better? How then will we find happiness in heaven?

Activities

God created heaven and earth. One point of contact between you and heaven is your guardian angel. Speak to your angel about your life up to this point and about your hopes for heaven.

God gives grace to believe. Ask God for that grace. Read Romans 11:33-36, and then reflect on God's creative power and providential wisdom as you have experienced them.

Chapter Four

JESUS CHRIST

An atheist was giving the old pastor a hard time. "Having a Church sounds like a good way to become famous. Maybe I should start one myself." "No problem," replied the pastor with a smile, "just get yourself crucified....Then rise from the dead on the third day!"

"I believe in Jesus Christ, his only Son, our Lord"

The Church's annual celebration of Easter declares that Jesus Christ, through his life, death, and Resurrection, is the founder of our Catholic Church. The purpose of the *Catechism*—and of Catholicism itself—is to bring people into communion with Jesus Christ. Everything else is taught in reference to him. So we must know what our faith teaches about Jesus, and to this end the *Catechism* explains the principal titles given to him (C 422-429).

The name *Jesus* means "God saves." Jesus came to save us from our sins, to give us salvation, which is the life of God's grace here and eternal happiness with God in heaven. Only God can forgive sins, so the name Jesus signifies that God is present to us in Jesus. The name of Jesus has been exalted above every other name, and it is at the heart of Christian prayer (C 430-435).

The name *Christ* comes from the Greek word for the Hebrew *messiah*, meaning "anointed." Jesus is the fulfillment of Old Testament prophecies foretelling a Messiah who as king, priest, and prophet would save people from sin. He was anointed by the Father with the Holy Spirit (Acts of the Apostles 10:38). Jesus accepted the title of Messiah in the presence of his apostles, but he did not allow it to be applied to him publicly because his contemporaries expected the Messiah to be a political ruler. The true meaning of Messiah was revealed when Jesus died and rose for our sins. Since then, the Church has recognized him as Messiah, as Christ (C 436-440).

Son of God is an expression applied uniquely to Jesus, who was proclaimed as God's beloved Son at his baptism and again at his Transfiguration. Jesus is the only Son of God and was acclaimed as such by the apostles after his Resurrection (John 3:16; C 441-445).

Lord is a title used for God in the Old Testament. Jesus is called Lord in the New Testament, and his divinity is announced when Thomas worships him with the words, "My Lord and my God!" (John 20:28). Because Jesus is Lord, the Church believes that he is the key, center, and purpose of human history (C 446-455).

The Incarnation

God's Son became human to save us from sin by reconciling us with God, to bring us God's love, to be for us a model of holiness, and to give us a share in God's own life by making us children of God (C 456-460).

Incarnation refers to the fact that the Son of God took on a human nature to bring about our salvation. Belief in the Incarnation is the distinctive sign of Christian faith (C 461-463).

Jesus Christ is truly God and truly human. From the beginning the Church has held this belief and defended it against heresies (false teachings) that denied it. The heresy of Gnostic Docetism denied that Jesus had a real physical body. Arianism claimed that Jesus was not truly God. Nestorianism asserted that the divine person was joined to a human person in Christ. The Monophysites contended that Christ's human nature ceased to exist when the divine person assumed it. Against these heresies the Church professed that Jesus Christ has two natures, divine and human, united in one divine person. He became truly human without ever ceasing to be God (C 464-469).

Jesus has both a human body and a human soul, with human intellect and will. Therefore, in his mortal life on earth, he had human knowledge, which was limited: Scripture says that he grew in wisdom and age. Because his human nature was united to the divine person, however, Christ had a special awareness of his status as Son of the Father, an ability to see into human hearts, and an understanding of God's plans. Christ had a human will that was perfectly attuned with his divine will. He had a real body, which made God visible. He had human emotions and a heart full of love for us (C 470-483).

"He was conceived by the power of the Holy Spirit and born of the Virgin Mary"

At the Annunciation, Mary was invited to become the mother of the Savior. When she asked how this could happen, she was told that the Holy Spirit would come over her so that Jesus would be miraculously conceived in her womb (C 484-486).

The Church's teachings about Mary and its belief in Christ are closely interrelated. Mary was chosen by God to be the mother of Christ. Her special place in history was prefigured by many holy women in the Old Testament. She was prepared by God to be Christ's mother through the privilege of the Immaculate Conception. From the moment of her own conception, Mary was redeemed from sin by the anticipated merits of Christ, and so the angel Gabriel addressed her as "full of grace." With the help of God's grace, she remained free from sin throughout her life (C 487-493).

When Mary responded to Gabriel, "Let it be done," Jesus Christ was conceived in her womb. The second Person of the Trinity took on flesh. Therefore, Mary is truly the mother of God. Because the conception was miraculous, Mary remained a virgin, fulfilling a prophecy in Isaiah 7:14 that a virgin would conceive and bear a son. This conception is history, not legend. Because it was met with incredulity by nonbelievers, it could not have been invented to win people over. It is reality, accessible only to faith (C 494-498).

Mary was married to Joseph, a carpenter of Nazareth, but she remained ever a virgin. Those called the brothers and sisters of Jesus in the Gospels are cousins or disciples. Some of them are identified as children of another woman, and the Bible never speaks of other children of Mary (Matthew 13:55; 27:56). Mary's virginity is testimony to the divinity of Jesus, for God was his only Father and he—Jesus—was conceived by the Spirit. Mary's virginity is a sign of her faith. It makes her a symbol of the Church, which also brings forth children for God through Baptism by the Holy Spirit's power (C 499-511).

The Mysteries of Christ's Life

The Creed says little about Christ's life, focusing instead on the principal mysteries of salvation. The Gospels proclaim Jesus as savior of the world, telling only those facts necessary for this purpose. But everything Christ did and said was intended to reveal the Father to us, to win our redemption from sin, and to restore us to our original status as God's children. Whatever Christ did, he did for us. He is our model. He enables us to live in him, and he lives in us (C 512-521).

Christ's Infancy and Hidden Life

Christ's coming was announced by the prophets, the last one being John the Baptist. Each year the Advent liturgy recalls how humankind waited for the Messiah, and it proclaims that Christ will come again. Advent leads to Christmas, when we celebrate Christ's Nativity. Born into a poor family in a stable at Bethlehem and visited by humble shepherds, Jesus invites us to become humble children of God and to allow him to be born in us (C 522-526).

Jesus demonstrated his submission to the law of Israel when he was circumcised on the eighth day after his birth. His mission to every nation was manifested when he was visited by the wise men from the East, an event recalled at Epiphany. He was presented in the Temple according to Jewish law and was recognized by Simeon and Anna as the savior of Israel. But he was rejected by King Herod and escaped death only by going into exile in Egypt with Mary and Joseph (C 527-530).

After Herod's death the family returned to their home at Nazareth. Here Jesus remained, obedient to Mary and Joseph, living simply, doing manual labor, inviting us to be united with him in the ordinary circumstances of daily life. His pilgrimage to Jerusalem at age twelve, the one event related about Jesus' years at Nazareth, manifested his desire to be in his Father's house, doing his Father's work (C 531-534).

Jesus' Public Life

Jesus' public life began when he was baptized by John in the Jordan River; he, though sinless, thereby signified his oneness with us, who are sinners. Jesus next fasted for forty days in the wilderness, defeating Satan's attempts to distract him from his mission. He then began to preach in Galilee, announcing the coming of God's kingdom, inviting all, even sinners, to accept it with humble hearts. His invitation came in the form of parables urging people to give everything to gain God's kingdom. He supported his teaching by miracles that invited belief and by his power over demons (C 535-550).

Jesus chose twelve apostles to share his ministry. He gave a special place to Simon Peter as the rock on which he would build his Church and to whom he would give the power of the keys to govern that Church. After Peter acclaimed Jesus as the Christ, Jesus began to explain that he would sacrifice his life for the world. Glory, symbolized in the Transfiguration, could come only through the cross (C 551-556).

Jesus' mission met with opposition from those who would not put faith in him as Messiah. As his preaching drew to a close, Jesus went to Jerusalem, knowing that his enemies would confront him. Enthusiastic followers acclaimed him, but Jesus, by riding on a donkey, showed that he came to conquer sin, not with violence, but with humility (C 557-570).

"He suffered under Pontius Pilate, was crucified, died, and was buried"

Jesus came to Jerusalem for the Passover feast, recalling how the Jews once passed over from slavery in Egypt to freedom in the Promised Land. Jesus' own Passover from death to new life accomplished our salvation (C 571-573).

Jesus was threatened with death because some Jewish leaders felt he was an agent of Satan. They believed that he opposed the Law, the Temple, and belief in one God. Jesus came to fulfill the Law, but to do this he had to correct false interpretations given by the Pharisees. Jesus loved the Temple and drove merchants from its outer courts (thus enraging officials who profited from Temple commerce), but he knew it would be destroyed and could not remain a focal point for true worship. Jesus taught that there is only one God, but he identified himself with God in his power to forgive sins. Jesus' approach to the Law, the Temple, and belief in God thereby became grounds for the charge of blasphemy leveled against him (C 574-594).

Those who plotted against Jesus included Pharisees zealous for the Law, members of Herod's party, and wealthy Sadducees of the priestly class who feared that Jesus might cause an uprising against the Romans. The Sanhedrin, the Jewish high court, made the final decision against Jesus. Therefore, Jesus' death cannot be blamed on the Jewish people as a whole, but on the leaders who opposed him and on all who are sinners (C 595-598).

Christ's death fit into God's plan for our salvation and was foretold in Old Testament prophecies. That God sent the Son to live among sinners for their redemption is proof of God's love for us (C 599-605).

God's love found perfect human expression in Jesus' readiness to do God's will. Even when Jesus' love for us began to lead inevitably to the cross, he did not turn back. God is love, and no one could have greater love than willingly to lay down one's life for one's friends (John 15:13). On the night before he died, at the Last Supper, Jesus expressed his willingness to sacrifice his life. In his agony at the garden of Gethsemani, he overcame human fear and embraced the Father's will. He then gave his life for us, his obedience replacing our disobedience. As God and as a human being, he embraced all people. By giving his life he became the head of humanity, the unique mediator between God and us forever. He invites us to unite our sufferings to his, as Mary did when she joined willingly in the mystery of his redemptive death (C 606-623).

When we say that Christ died and was buried, we mean that his human soul was separated from his body. Both body and soul, however, remained joined to his divine person, and God's power saved his body from corruption as it awaited Easter. We are united to Christ's death by Baptism, as we die to sin that we may rise to new life (C 624-630).

"He descended into hell.
On the third day he rose again."

The word *hell* in the Creed is an ancient usage which denotes not a place of punishment, but the abode of the dead. To say that Jesus descended into hell means that he truly died to be with those holy souls who were awaiting the fullness of life. His death made it possible for them and for people of every age to attain perfect happiness in heaven (C 631-637).

Christ did not remain among the dead. On the third day after his crucifixion, followers discovered that his tomb was empty. Then Jesus appeared to Mary Magdalene and other women, to his apostles, and to hundreds of others. His followers, at first incredulous, soon became convinced of the reality of his Resurrection. Christ's appearances to his followers proved that he had returned to them in the same body that had died on the cross. Yet it was glorious, with remarkable powers, immune to suffering and death, free from the limits of space and time. He had not returned to this mortal life in a mortal body (as Lazarus did), but he had passed through death to the perfection of human life. This is a mystery we cannot entirely grasp, a marvelous intervention of Father, Son, and Holy Spirit in human history (C 638-650).

The Resurrection confirmed everything Jesus had taught and done. It demonstrated the reality of the Incarnation. It opened the way to eternal life for us. It conquered sin, for it allowed everyone who follows Christ to overcome death. Because Christ died, we, too, shall rise! (C 651-658).

"He ascended into heaven
and is seated at the right hand of the Father."

The New Testament records that for forty days Jesus appeared to his followers, teaching and encouraging them. Then he ascended into heaven on a cloud to God's right hand, signifying that his humanity would forever share in divine glory. Christ is where God is…everywhere, and he remains with his Church always (C 659-667).

"He will come again
to judge the living and the dead."

In heaven, Jesus Christ is Lord of the universe and of human history. He is head of the Church and dwells in the Church. At the end of time (exactly when this will be is unknown), Christ will come again. Then evil will be completely vanquished, and God will reign over "new heavens and a new earth" (2 Peter 3:13). Now we are in the final age of the Church, a time to work with Christ for the establishment of his kingdom. Trials still test us, and Scripture speaks of tribulation that will cause many to fall away. But Jesus is Lord, and he cannot be overcome. He will judge all people to the degree that they have imitated him in love of God and neighbor (C 668-682).

*Christ established his Church by his life, death, and Resurrection. He is **Jesus**, our Savior, who invites us to be on a "first-name" basis with him; he calls us friends (John 15:15). He is **Christ**, the Anointed, the only one who can give meaning to life. He is **Son of God**, who allows us to become God's children. He is **Lord**, truly God, who offers us the grace of God's love now and forever.*

Questions for Discussion or Reflection

On the night before he died, Jesus said to the apostles—and to us, "You are my friends." Is Jesus a personal friend to you? Do you believe that he loves you so much that he would die for your salvation alone? Do you allow him to influence the daily decisions you make about your family, social life, work, and recreation?

Activities

Reflect on the titles given to Jesus. Talk to Jesus as the savior who wants to be on a "first-name" basis with you. Ask him as Christ to give real meaning to your life. Thank him, the Son of God, for making you God's child. Adore him as Lord, and pray that one day you may see him, face to face, in heaven.

Chapter Five

THE HOLY SPIRIT
AND THE CHURCH

On Pentecost the Holy Spirit descended upon the apostles in wind and tongues of fire. If this happened to a modern congregation—with today's concerns about fire safety—the ushers would probably run for the extinguishers!

Many people find it easier to relate to God as Father and to Jesus as Brother than to the Holy Spirit. But the *Catechism* can help us understand that the wind and fire of the Spirit are as close as the air we breathe and the love that warms our hearts.

"I believe in the Holy Spirit"

Those who believe in Jesus have been touched by the Holy Spirit, for no one can say Jesus is Lord without the Spirit's help (1 Corinthians 12:3). The Spirit gives us grace to know Jesus as Lord and God as Father. The Spirit is one of the persons of the Trinity, equal to Father and Son, and works in the Church for our salvation (C 683-686).

The Father is known through the works of creation, and the Son through his redemptive works. The Holy Spirit is known through works accomplished in the Church: Scripture and sacred Tradition, the Church's magisterium (teaching office), sacramental liturgy, prayer, charisms, ministries, apostolic life, and saints (C 687-688).

The Joint Mission of the Son and the Spirit

Father, Son, and Holy Spirit are one. The Father sends Son and Spirit together, distinct but inseparable. Jesus is called *Christ* because he was anointed with the Spirit. After Jesus' Ascension, he sent the Spirit upon his followers, enabling them to live in union with him (C 689-690).

Names, Titles, and Symbols of the Holy Spirit

Spirit translates the Hebrew word *ruah*, meaning "breath, air, or wind." *Holy Spirit* is the proper name for the third Person of the Trinity (C 691).

Jesus gave the Holy Spirit the title of Paraclete (Advocate), meaning "called to one's side" or "consoler." Other titles in the New Testament include Spirit of the promise, Spirit of adoption, Spirit of Christ, Spirit of the Lord, Spirit of God, and Spirit of glory (C 692-693).

The name *Holy Spirit* carries the symbolism of breath and wind. Many other symbols in Scripture signify the Spirit. Water bespeaks the Spirit's life-giving action in Baptism. Anointing with oil intimates the Spirit, who anointed Christ and now anoints believers. Fire, transforming what it touches, is a sign of the Spirit. Cloud and light symbolize the Holy Spirit, as at the Transfiguration when a bright cloud overshadowed Jesus. Other symbols include the seal, the healing hand of Jesus, the finger of God, and the dove (C 694-701).

The Holy Spirit and the Old Covenant

The Holy Spirit and Jesus are not fully revealed in the Old Testament, but they are promised and foreshadowed. At Creation, God's Word (Son) brought everything into being, and the Breath (Spirit) of God animated living creatures. Humanity, created in God's image, was disfigured by sin and lost its God-given glory. But God promised to remake us in the divine image through the Son and restore us to glory through the Spirit. God kept the promises alive by theophanies (self-revelations) like the appearance to Moses at the burning bush. God guided people toward Christ through the Law, and when the Jewish nation was exiled because of disobedience, God brought back a remnant to the Promised Land as a foreshadowing of the Church. God gave hope through prophecies of a Messiah who, by accepting suffering and death, would pour out his Spirit on humanity. These prophecies were fulfilled in Jesus, the Suffering Servant, and in the outpouring of the Spirit at Pentecost (C 702-716).

The Holy Spirit in the "Fullness of Time"

The work of preparing humanity for the Messiah was completed by John the Baptist. Filled with the Spirit, he pointed people toward Jesus, who would baptize with water and the Spirit (C 717-20).

Jesus came into the world through Mary. She was perfectly prepared by the Holy Spirit to be the mother of God's Son. Conceived without sin, Mary was a fitting dwelling place for Son and Spirit. The Spirit descended upon Mary, enabling her to make God's Word visible when she conceived Christ by the Holy Spirit's power. Through Mary the Spirit brought people—first the shepherds, then all believers—to Jesus. At Christ's death, Mary was revealed as the Woman, the new Eve who is mother of Christ's disciples. She, as Mother of the Church, prayed with the apostles after Christ's Ascension while they awaited the coming of the Spirit (C 721-726).

The fundamental mission of the Holy Spirit was the anointing of Jesus as Christ-Messiah, who then gradually revealed the Spirit in his teaching. Jesus, shortly before his death, promised to send the Spirit to be with the Church forever and to lead it to all truth. Jesus appeared to his apostles on Easter, breathing the Spirit upon them so they might forgive sins. At that moment, the mission of Jesus and the Spirit became the mission of the Church (C 727-730).

The Holy Spirit and the Church in the "Last Days"

When Jesus sent the Spirit at Pentecost, he fully revealed the Trinity and invited all to become members of the Church. This signaled the era known as the "last days," the era of the Church that will endure until Christ comes at the end of time (C 731-732).

Christ's gift of the Spirit is a gift of love. This gift brings forgiveness, replacing the death of sin with God's life, enabling us to love with God's love and to bear the "fruit of the Spirit" described in Galatians 5:22-23 (C 733-36).

The mission of Christ and the Spirit is completed by the Church, the Body of Christ and Temple of the Spirit. The Spirit prepares us to receive Christ, reveals Christ, and unites us with Christ. The Church is a sacrament, a sign, bringing Christ to the world. Through the seven sacraments of the Church, Christ's Spirit and life are communicated to members of his Body (Part Two of the *Catechism*). The Church helps us to live as Christ teaches (Part Three). Guided by the Spirit, as members of the Church, we pray in union with Christ (Part Four) (C 737-747).

"The holy catholic Church"

We believe in a Church whose purpose is to bring Christ's light to the world, a Church that always depends on the Spirit as its source of holiness. What we believe about the Church is based on our faith in God the Father, Son, and Holy Spirit (C 748-750).

Names, Images, and Symbols of the Church

The word *church* means "convocation" or "assembly." In the Old Testament it was applied to the Chosen People. When believers in Jesus called themselves a Church, they showed that their community was now God's Chosen People. Today the word *Church* refers to the gathering of believers at liturgy, to local parish churches, and to the universal community of believers. The Bible explains the Church by many titles and symbols: the people of God, Body of Christ, sheepfold, cultivated field or vineyard, God's building, God's family and temple, Jerusalem above, our mother, and spouse of Christ (C 751-757).

The Church's Origin, Foundation, and Mission

God planned from eternity that humanity should be joined to God through Christ. God prepared the world by forming Israel as a people, and Jesus accomplished God's plan by preaching the Good News of God's kingdom. Those who welcome Jesus are gathered around him as his Church. Jesus gave that Church a structure by choosing the twelve apostles, with Peter as their head. He gave the Church life through his death and Resurrection. He revealed the Church to the world by sending the Spirit on Pentecost. The Spirit guides the Church and bestows the charismatic and organizational gifts needed to proclaim the Gospel. The Church fulfills its mission amid trials and persecutions and will reach perfection only at the end of time (C 758-769).

The Mystery of the Church

The Greek word *mysterion* is translated into Latin by the words *mysterium* and *sacramentum*. *Sacrament* signifies the visible sign of the hidden reality of salvation, which is indicated by the word *mystery*. The Church is a *mystery* for many reasons. It exists in history, yet goes beyond history. It has a hierarchical structure, but is the Mystical Body of Christ. It is visible, yet spiritual. It exists in heaven, as well as on earth. Christ is present in the Church, where we have communion with God through holiness of life in imitation of Mary, model of the Church (C 770-773).

The Church is a *sacrament* in the sense that it is a visible sign of the hidden reality of salvation. The Church makes Christ visible and signifies our union with God and with one another. The seven sacraments are special signs and instruments through which God bestows Christ's grace within the Church (C 774-780).

The Church—People of God

God saves human beings not as individuals without any connection to one another, but as a people. Having prepared the world by forming a covenant with the Israelites, God invited all humanity to be a people saved by Christ and united in the Holy Spirit. This people belongs to God through faith and Baptism. Its head is Jesus Christ, and its members are God's children. Its law is the new commandment to love as Christ does. Its mission is to be light for the world. Its destiny is the kingdom of God begun on earth and perfected in heaven. Since Jesus was priest, prophet, and king, his followers are to be a priestly, prophetic, and royal people by worshiping God, witnessing the Good News, and serving others (C 781-786).

The Church—Body of Christ

Jesus invited his followers to intimate union with him and with all believers; he is the vine of which we are the branches. Through the Eucharist he lives in us and we in him. He promised to be with us forever, and he sent the Spirit to make us his Body. By Baptism and Eucharist, we are united with one another as Christ's Mystical Body, without losing our individual gifts or diversities. Christ is the head of this Body, associating us with his suffering, death, and Resurrection and providing for our growth, so that we become with him one mystical person. At the same time, a real distinction remains between Christ and us, expressed in the image of Christ as bridegroom and Church as bride (C 787-796).

The Church—Temple of the Holy Spirit

The Holy Spirit is the "soul" of Christ's Mystical Body, dwelling in Head and members, making us one. The Spirit works through the sacraments, grace, the virtues, and through charisms—gifts of service to be used by individuals for the good of others under the guidance of the Church's leaders (C 797-810).

Marks of the Church

The Church is one, holy, catholic, and apostolic. These four characteristics are essential features of the Church and have been manifested throughout its history. They help us to recognize the Church as Christ's Body (C 811-812).

The Church Is One

The Church is one because its source is the one God, its founder is Christ, and its soul is the Holy Spirit. There is diversity within the Church, but its members are unified by the bond of charity, by one profession of faith, by a common worship, and by the apostolic succession of bishops. The true Church of Jesus Christ subsists in the Catholic Church, for it is only here that the *fullness* of the means of salvation can be obtained and only here that the college (assembly) of bishops exists under the successor of Peter (C 813-816).

Throughout history the Church has suffered from divisions arising from heresy (denial of essential truths), apostasy (total renunciation of the Faith), and schism (breaking away from unity). Some divisions have resulted in the separation of large communities from the Church, often due to fault on both sides. Members born into such communities today cannot be charged with the sin of separation, and the Church regards them as brothers and sisters. Justified by faith and Baptism, they are incorporated into Christ. Their churches contain many elements of sanctification and truth, and the Spirit uses them as means of salvation (C 817-819).

Christ called for perfect unity among his followers, and we should respond by renewal, conversion of heart, common prayer, knowledge of one another, ecumenical formation, dialogue, and collaboration in works of charity. Since perfect unity transcends human abilities, we place our trust in Christ who alone can make us one (C 820-822).

The Church Is Holy

The Church is holy because it is loved by Christ, its head. Joined to God, who gives it the fullness of the means of salvation, the Church exists to make human beings holy. The holiness of the Church on earth is real though imperfect, and we must constantly strive for holiness, trying to imitate the love of Christ. He is sinless, but he accepts us into the Church as sinners that we may follow the path of penance and renewal. In our striving, we have the saints, especially the Virgin Mary, as models of holiness, virtue, and fidelity (C 823-829).

The Church Is Catholic

Catholic means universal. The Church is catholic because Christ is present with all the graces necessary for salvation, and because the Church is sent to the whole human race. Each particular church—each diocese under its bishop—is catholic because of its union with the Church of Rome. The Church finds its home in a variety of cultures, disciplines, liturgical rites, and heritages (C 830-835).

Full membership in the Church comes from acceptance of all its beliefs and sacraments and from union with the pope and bishops. The Church has a real, if imperfect, unity with Orthodox Churches and with baptized non-Catholics. It is related to people who believe in God—to the Jews with whom we share the Old Covenant (Testament), to Muslims who profess the faith of Abraham, and to other non-Christian religions. Those who, through no fault of their own, do not have an explicit knowledge of Christ can achieve salvation if they try, assisted by God's grace, to lead good lives; their salvation comes from Christ even though they do not know him. Those who culpably reject Christ and his Church, however, forfeit eternal life, and in this sense it is true to say that outside the Church there is no salvation (C 836-848).

Christ asks the Church to preach the Gospel to the world. This mandate springs from God's love; its purpose is to unite every person to God. The Church, out of love, guided by the Spirit, imitates Christ in the process of evangelization. Struggling against human weakness, the Church patiently unites itself to humanity as it preaches to nonbelievers, establishes Christian communities, and forms local churches. It works toward Christian unity and maintains a respectful dialogue with those who do not accept the Gospel (C 849-856).

The Church Is Apostolic

The Church is apostolic because it is built on the foundation of the twelve apostles, hands on their teaching, and is guided by them and their successors. *Apostle* means "emissary" (someone who is sent), and Christ sent the apostles to continue his mission. He promised to be with them until the end of time, so they appointed bishops as successors to continue their work. The entire Church, in union with the bishops and pope, is apostolic because all its members share in Christ's mission in various ways. The success of their apostolate depends on their union with Christ, the gifts of the Spirit, and charity drawn from the Eucharist. The Church—one, holy, catholic, and apostolic—strives to establish the kingdom of God on earth, always trusting that Christ's love will finally bring it to perfection, making it his bride in heaven (C 857-870).

The Book of Revelation says that the Spirit and the bride beckon us (22:17). The Spirit's breath of life and fire of love encourage us to live as members of Christ's Church on earth so that we may be one with Christ forever in heaven.

Questions for Discussion or Reflection

The *Catechism* gives many names, titles, and symbols of the Holy Spirit and the Church. Which are most meaningful to you? Why?

The Church is the Mystical Body of Christ; what does this mean to you?

How can you personally make the Church more one, holy, catholic, and apostolic?

Activities

At the Last Supper Jesus promised to send the Holy Spirit to dwell within us. (See John 14:15-17.) Reflect on the presence of the Spirit within you, and speak to the Spirit as your Advocate and Consoler.

Chapter Six

LIFE HERE
AND LIFE EVERLASTING

A circus high-wire performer sought a volunteer from the audience. A young man came forward and was asked, "Do you believe I can ride my bicycle across that wire fifty feet above the ring, without a safety net?" "Beats me," replied the volunteer. The performer raced up a ladder, hopped on his bike, zoomed across the wire at breathtaking speed, did a U-turn, and zipped back. He called to the volunteer, "Do you believe that I can do it blindfolded?" "Sure," said the volunteer enthusiastically. "If you can do what you just did, you can do anything!" "Great," replied the performer, tying on a blindfold. "Now climb up and hop on the handlebars!"

...Oops. It's easy to believe in someone as long as we don't have to risk our own neck. But real faith in another means that we are willing to be personally involved. When Jesus was arrested, his apostles ran away. Later, convinced by his Resurrection, they gladly joined his "act," believing that he would bring them through danger and death to eternal life.

The *Catechism* continues its explanation of the Church by showing how faith includes real involvement and personal commitment to Jesus. Faith may at times put us on a "high wire," but it offers Christ's guarantee of eternal life!

Christ's Faithful

What does it mean to be a Christian? It means to be a sharer in Christ's priestly (sanctifying), prophetic (teaching), and kingly (governing) office and to carry out the mission God has entrusted to the Church. It means commitment to the cause for which Christ came into this world. Through Baptism all the faithful are equal in dignity and in the work they do to build up the Body of Christ. There are different ministries in the Church, all contributing to its unity of mission. Christ has entrusted the office of teaching, sanctifying, and governing to the apostles and their successors, the hierarchy. Christ gives the laity a share in this office and an assignment in the mission of the Church. He calls some from both hierarchy and laity to consecrate themselves to God through the evangelical counsels; they form the religious communities and institutes whose members take vows or make other forms of commitment to God in the Church (C 871-873).

The Hierarchical Constitution of the Church

A hierarchy is a governing body of individuals organized into orders, each subordinate to the one above. Catholics believe that Christ instituted the Church with its authority, mission, orientation, and goal. The hierarchy (order of ministers) in the Church, therefore, comes from Christ, who alone can authorize people to preach and baptize in his name. Grace comes, not from ourselves, but from God through those whom God sends (Romans 10:14-15). Christ empowers ministers to do and give by God's grace what they could not do and give on their own. Their mission is linked to Christ's and accordingly must be a ministry of *service* (1 Corinthians 9:19). This ministry is *collegial*, for Christ sent the apostles together, not independently. In imitation of them, bishops are joined to one another in communion with the pope, and priests exercise ministry as a group under the direction of their proper bishop. At the same time, ministry must be *personal*, for each is called personally by Christ (C 874-879).

The Bishops and the Pope

Christ summoned the apostles as the "Twelve," as a college, in the sense of a body or permanent assembly. He placed Peter at their head. Peter's successor is the pope, and the successors of the apostles are the bishops, so their pastoral office comes from Christ. The pope is vicar of Christ, meaning that he is a sign of Christ's presence, acting in Christ's name as pastor. He exercises authority over the whole Church, showing that the Church is one. The college of bishops, united to the pope, also has authority over the universal Church; it exercises this authority solemnly at ecumenical councils recognized by the pope. The college of bishops, united under the pope, demonstrates the Church's variety, universality, and unity. Individual bishops lead their local churches, or dioceses, assisted by priests and deacons. They also share concern for all other churches, for the poor and persecuted, and for missionaries. Neighboring dioceses form ecclesiastical provinces, patriarchates, or regions. Bishops may meet in synods or provincial councils as a way of cooperating with one another (C 880-887).

The first task of bishops and priests is *teaching*, preaching the Gospel. The truth taught by Christ must be brought to the world. To preserve the Church in his truth, Christ has given the Church the charism, or gift, of infallibility. This charism is exercised by the pope when, as pastor of all the faithful, he proclaims by a definitive act a doctrine pertaining to faith or morals. It is exercised by the bishops when in union with the pope—most notably at an ecumenical council—they propose doctrine as divinely revealed. To all *infallible* statements we owe the *assent (obedience) of faith,* for such statements have the special seal of Christ's Holy Spirit. To papal and episcopal *noninfallible* teachings which lead to a clearer understanding of Revelation, we owe *religious assent.* (Infallible statements are rare. An example of an infallible papal definition is the declaration of Mary's Assumption in 1950.) Refusal to give the assent of faith is heresy. Refusal to give religious assent, while it might involve a lack of faith, is not necessarily heretical (C 888-893).

The second task of bishops and priests is *sanctifying* the Church. They do this through their ministry of word and sacraments, especially the Eucharist, and by their prayer, work, and good example (C 893).

The third task is *governing.* Bishops rule and guide the Church with authority that comes from Christ. They, as well as the priests and deacons who assist them, should lead with compassion and understanding, for their model is Christ, the Good Shepherd (C 894-96).

The Lay Faithful

Lay faithful, or laity, here refers to members of the Church who are not ordained or committed by vows to religious life. Most Catholics (over 99.5 percent) are laity, and the success of Christ's mission in the world depends largely on them. They are the "front line" of Church life. Their role is to bring Christ into the world—into the social, political, and economic realms of human existence. By Baptism and Confirmation they have the right and duty to convey the message of salvation. Many people will come to know Christ only through the laity. Without the cooperation of the laity, the apostolate of ordained ministers cannot be fully effective (C 897-900).

Laypeople share in the *priestly* office of Christ by joining their lives—work, family relationships, prayer, apostolic endeavors, relaxation, hardships—to Christ's and by offering them to God in the Eucharist. Parents share in Christ's priestly work by a holy married life and by leading their children to Christ. Laypeople can be admitted to the ministries of lector and acolyte. In case of necessity, the laity can serve as readers, leaders at liturgical prayer, and as ministers of Baptism and Holy Communion (C 901-903).

Laypeople participate in Christ's *prophetic* office by giving good example and by telling others about Jesus. With proper training, they may serve as catechists, teachers of sacred sciences (theology), and religious media specialists. They have the right and duty to express their opinion to pastors and others about matters which pertain to the good of the Church (C 904-907).

Laypeople exercise Christ's *kingly* office by overcoming the slavery of sin in themselves and in the world, so that God's freedom and justice may reign. They may serve the Church by exercising different ministries and by taking part in governing bodies, such as parish councils, finance committees, and church tribunals. They must try to harmonize their duties as members of the Church and of human society, remembering that all actions fall under God's dominion (C 908-913).

The Consecrated Life

Consecrated life is a permanent state characterized by profession of the evangelical counsels of chastity, poverty, and obedience. In the religious state, men and women strive toward perfection in a self-dedication rooted in Baptism. Since the time of Christ, many forms of consecrated life have developed to serve the Church and to promote holiness. The life of a *hermit* involves devotion to solitude and prayer, which demonstrates the importance of intimacy with Christ. *Consecrated virginity* is a state whereby women commit themselves to God and serve the Church in various ways individually or in associations. *Religious life* is distinguished from other kinds of consecrated life by its liturgical character, public vows, communal life, and unique witness to Christ's union with the Church. Religious collaborate with their diocesan bishop in his pastoral duties. *Secular institutes* are associations of people who strive for perfection and work for the sanctification of the world from within. *Societies of apostolic life* are those which, without the public vows of religious communities, share life in common to achieve a particular apostolic purpose; they may embrace the evangelical counsels (vows) according to their constitution. All those who live some form of consecrated life show Christ's presence in the Church and serve the Church's mission. They encourage others by their example and show that our true goal is heaven (C 914-945).

"The communion of saints"

Since the Church is the Body of Christ, any goodness in one part of the Body is communicated to all, just as nourishment in a physical body benefits the whole organism. The grace that comes from the most important member, Christ, is communicated to us through the sacraments. Thus the *communion of saints* (*communio sanctorum* in Latin) means that holy things (*sancta*) are communicated to God's holy people (*sancti*). The things shared include faith, sacraments, charisms (spiritual gifts), material possessions, and works of charity (C 946-953).

The Church includes people in three states of life: those here on earth, those being purified after death (in purgatory), and those in heaven. Through the communion of saints, all can share spiritual goods. The saints in heaven pray for us on earth; union with them brings us closer to Christ. We pray for those who are being purified after death, and they intercede (pray) for us. By love and prayer, we are one family under God, one holy Catholic Church (C 954-962).

Mary—Mother of Christ, Mother of the Church

Mary, Mother of Christ, is mother of the members of Christ's Body. She was closely joined to her Son's life and death, and from the cross Jesus gave her as mother to every beloved disciple. After Jesus' Ascension, Mary prayed with other believers for the coming of the Holy Spirit and so helped the Church at its beginnings. Her Assumption was a unique participation in her Son's Resurrection and a sign of hope to all (C 963-966).

Because of her obedience to God and her devotion to Jesus, Mary is the perfect model of faith and charity. By her singular cooperation in Christ's redemptive work, she is a mother to us in the order of grace. What she began on earth she continues in heaven as our Advocate, Helper, Benefactress, and Mediatrix. Of course, she is subordinate to Christ; he is uniquely the mediator between God and us. But God shares grace through others, especially through Mary. Therefore, the Church rightly honors her in obedience to Scripture with devotion that differs essentially from the adoration given to God (Luke 1:48). We venerate her as a perfect model of what the Church should be (C 967-975).

"The forgiveness of sins"

The Apostles' Creed connects belief in the forgiveness of sins to belief in the Holy Spirit, the Church, and the communion of saints. On Easter Sunday evening Jesus breathed the Holy Spirit upon the apostles and gave them the power to forgive sins in his name (John 20:22-23). Jesus associated forgiveness with Baptism, which frees a person from original sin, personal sins, and any punishment due him or her. Weaknesses of nature still remain, however, and Christ gave the Church the sacrament of Penance to free us from sins committed after Baptism. Christ granted the power to forgive sins, the power of the keys, to the apostles and their successors. He desires that the news of this gift and of God's readiness to forgive be brought to the world (C 976-987).

"The resurrection of the body"

The Creed proclaims our belief that we continue to live after death. The people of the Old Covenant gradually came to a realization of life everlasting, expressed in later books of the Old Testament such as 2 Maccabees, Daniel, and Wisdom. The Pharisees and many other Jews of Jesus' time believed in resurrection, and Jesus taught it as certain. He associated belief in bodily resurrection with belief in himself, the "resurrection and the life" (John 11:25). After Christ's Resurrection, believers linked faith in him with our resurrection to eternal life (C 988-996).

In 1 Corinthians 15, Saint Paul teaches that the dead will rise. We pass through death to eternal life: The soul lives on through death, and the body is transformed into a "spiritual body." New life is given now, at the moment of death, and at the end of time. Through Baptism we have died to sin and *now* live a new life with Christ. *At the moment of death,* we rise to a new stage of human life. *At the end of time,* our bodies are definitively reunited with our souls in some mysterious way which only God knows (C 997-1004).

We must die to live forever with Christ. Death as we know it is the consequence of sin, but it makes us realize the importance of human life: We have only a limited time to bring our lives to fulfillment. Moreover, death has been transformed by Christ. He accepted death freely and obediently. Since he died for us, we can die and rise with him. Death is our birth to eternal life, our pathway to God's presence. This vision of death is given expression in the Church's liturgy, and the Church encourages us to pray for a happy death. We ask Mary to intercede for us now and at the hour of our death. We entrust ourselves to Saint Joseph, the patron of a happy death (C 1005-1019).

"And the life everlasting"

The Church's belief in everlasting life is expressed in its prayers and in the sacraments ministered to the dying—Penance, Anointing of the Sick, and Eucharist (as Viaticum). Those who die meet Christ at the *particular judgment,* which occurs at the moment of death. In accordance with their faith and works, they move into the joys of heaven (immediately or after necessary purification) or into the condemnation of hell (C 1020-1021).

Those who die in God's grace, perfectly purified of sin, enter *heaven* to be with God, the saints, and the angels. Heaven is the happiness and fulfillment we seek. Made possible by the life, death, and Resurrection of Jesus, it involves joys which are suggested by many images of Scripture. The greatest joy of the saints is being in God's presence, seeing God face to face in the beatific vision, knowing that they have finally reached their goal, realizing that they can continue to bring about God's kingdom (C 1020-1029).

Those who die in God's friendship but who still need purification—from venial sin or from any punishment due to sin—enter the state known as *purgatory*. The exact nature of this purification is unknown. The Church speaks of a "purifying fire." (This cannot be simply a material fire since the soul is spiritual; above all it is the fire of God's love.) Belief in purgatory is based on the Bible's reference to a purification from sin after death and to the value of prayer for the deceased. To help those in purgatory, the Church recommends prayer, the Eucharist, almsgiving, indulgences, and works of penance (Matthew 12:31; 2 Maccabees 12:46; C 1030-1032).

To attain union with God in heaven, we must freely choose to love God. Those who, by mortal sin (see page 74), reject God's love and refuse to repent, separate themselves from God by their own free choice. This state of self-exclusion from God is known as hell. Jesus speaks of the terrible punishments of hell as eternal fire, and the Church has always taught the existence of hell. The worst punishment of *hell* is eternal separation from God, the only One who can give the happiness and peace we long for. God predestines no one to hell, and the Church prays in the liturgy that we will open our hearts to God's love and mercy (C 1033-1037).

At the end of time, all people will stand before Christ in a *Last Judgment*. This will not change the results of the particular judgment, but it will reveal to everyone the value of each person's life. Our lives have consequences, both good and bad, that continue after us, and it is only at the end of time that the story of each human's existence on earth will be complete. Only then can the fullness of God's justice and the greatness of God's plan be fully revealed. The Last Judgment bids us to make the most of our years on earth and to commit ourselves to God's kingdom (C 1038-1041).

Scripture teaches that at the end of time God's kingdom will come in its fullness and the universe will be renewed in "new heavens and a new earth" (2 Peter 3:13). This completion of God's plan will join us to God and to one another in perfect love. We will have a new relationship to God's creation and be able to appreciate God's magnificence manifested in created things. (Those who enjoy sightseeing are in for a real treat!) We do not know the time or exact manner of this new creation, but its certainty should encourage us to live and work with diligence and hope (C 1042-1060).

"Amen"

The Creed ends with the Hebrew word *amen*, which comes from the same root as *believe. Amen* expresses our trust in God and our belief in God's fidelity. Our lives should also be an "Amen" to our baptismal profession of faith. Finally, Christ is our "Amen," the fulfillment of all God's promises (Revelation 3:14; C 1061-1065).

And so we boldly step out on the "high wire" of life. We commit ourselves to Christ and to his mission, for we believe in life everlasting!

Questions for Discussion or Reflection

In the *Catechism's* explanation of what it means to be a Christian, is the emphasis on being saved by Christ or on being an active member of Christ's Church? Why?

What are some of the ways you exercise Christ's priestly, prophetic, and kingly offices?

Does death frighten you? Why or why not? What joys of heaven do you most anticipate?

Activities

Reflect on the saints in heaven and on the souls in purgatory who have believed the same truths we affirm in the Creed. Consider your union with them and with all believers on earth. As a member of this great communion of saints, pray the Apostles' Creed slowly, reverently, and gratefully.

Part Two

The
Celebration
of the Christian
Mystery

Chapter Seven

LITURGY AND THE SACRAMENTS OF INITIATION

"This is the Lamb of God," proclaims the priest, as he holds up the consecrated host. "Lord, I am not worthy," responds the congregation, as they prepare to receive Jesus in Holy Communion.

A notable feature of Catholicism is our belief in sacraments, physical signs which point to spiritual realities. The whole universe is a sign pointing to its Creator, and material things are good because they are formed by God, redeemed by Jesus Christ, and breathed upon by the Holy Spirit. Jesus taught that God touches us through created things. He used water, bread, wine, and oil to convey spiritual graces. He gave the Church the seven special signs we call the sacraments. Through them he continues to offer salvation to people of every age. Faith opens our eyes to see Christ and to meet him in the sacraments and liturgy of the Church.

Liturgy

The Creed proclaims that God the Father sent the Son and the Holy Spirit for our salvation. The paschal mystery of Christ's Passion, Resurrection, and Ascension gave life to the Church, and the Church celebrates this mystery in its liturgy (C 1066-1068).

Liturgy comes from a Greek word meaning "a public work" or "service on behalf of people." For Catholics, liturgy is our participation in Christ's work of redemption in, with, and through the Church. Liturgy gathers us as members of Christ's Body for ceremony and prayer by which we worship God, proclaim the Gospel, and serve our neighbor. Because liturgy is performed by the Mystical Body of Christ—Head and members—it is a sacred action which surpasses all others. It involves us in the life of the community and is a sign of our communion with God. It is a participation in Christ's own prayer to the Father in the Holy Spirit. It is the privileged place for catechesis as it leads us from the visible signs of sacraments to the invisible truths of Christian mysteries (C 1069-1075).

The Sacramental Economy

Christ revealed his Church at Pentecost and since then has acted through the Church's sacraments in what is called the "sacramental economy." "Economy" here has nothing to do with finance, but refers to the system or means by which Christ offers the graces of his paschal mystery (C 1076).

God the Father is the source of all blessings granted in the liturgy. These include everything God has said and done for us, from creation, through the Old Testament, to the salvation granted in Christ. The liturgy recalls and celebrates these blessings. The liturgy also allows us to "bless" God by acknowledging God's gifts with thanks and praise (C 1077-1083).

God the Son, the glorified Christ, is not limited by time or space, nor is the paschal mystery of his Passion, Resurrection, and Ascension. Unlike other historical events which remain in the past, Christ's paschal mystery is always present to us through the sacraments he instituted. These are signs—words and actions—which bestow the grace they signify. The sacraments are available to the Church because Christ made his apostles and their successors sacramental signs of himself. In every liturgical action Christ is truly present through the minister and the congregation. He speaks through Scripture and acts through the sacraments. He joins us to the saints and angels in worship and gives us a foretaste of our destiny in heaven (C 1084-1090).

God the Holy Spirit enables us to receive Christ's life in the liturgy in four special ways. First, the Spirit prepares us to receive Christ by recalling the attitudes of those who waited for the Savior. The Old Testament is proclaimed, the Psalms are prayed, and great events such as the Passover are remembered. We are thereby reminded to prepare ourselves to meet Christ today. Second, the Spirit calls to mind what Christ has done for us. The New Testament and that part of the liturgy called the *anamnesis* (remembering) recall what God has done for us and invite us to a living relationship with Christ. Third, the Spirit empowers us to participate in Christ's paschal mystery. Christ's Passion, Resurrection, and Ascension are not repeated, but made present. This is most obvious in the *epiclesis* prayer (the invocation) at Mass, when the priest asks the Father to send the Holy Spirit to change bread and wine into Christ's body and blood, allowing us to join Christ's offering of self to the Father. Fourth, the Spirit unites us to Christ and to one another, helping us to bring Christ's love to the world (C 1091-1112).

Paschal Mystery and Sacraments

The Church recognizes seven sacraments instituted by Christ: Baptism, Confirmation, Eucharist, Penance, Anointing of the Sick, Holy Orders, and Matrimony. What Christ did in his hidden and public life he now does through the sacraments, which are celebrated by the Church for members of the Church. The ordained priesthood ministers to the baptized priesthood—Christ's people—and guarantees by apostolic succession that it is Christ who acts through the sacraments. All sacraments bestow Christ's grace. Baptism, Confirmation, and Holy Orders also confer a sacramental character, or seal, which endures forever (C 1113-1121).

Christ sent his apostles to evangelize so that people might be baptized and receive the sacraments. The sacraments, as signs, instruct and strengthen faith. Because faith and liturgy are closely intertwined, the sacramental rite must not be changed arbitrarily (C 1122-1126).

Since Christ acts through the sacraments, they confer the grace they signify, grace necessary for salvation. As the sacraments bestow grace, they anticipate and pledge eternal life. The power of the sacraments depends on Christ, not the personal holiness of the minister or recipient. Nevertheless, the effects of the sacraments will depend in part on the dispositions of the one receiving them (C 1127-1134).

Celebration of the Liturgy

Since liturgy is the action of the whole Christ, those joined to Christ in heaven have a share in it as they worship God. Here on earth the liturgy is an action of the entire Church, and whenever possible, the sacraments ought to be celebrated communally. Members of the Church have different liturgical functions, for example, priest, readers, and choir, and they should carry out only those functions which pertain to their role (C 1135-1144).

Sacramental celebrations are made up of signs—words and actions—taken from visible creation, human life, the Old Covenant, and Christ himself. Music and singing are important parts of the liturgy; they invite community participation and add beauty and solemnity. Sacred images reflect the reality of the Incarnation. Images of Mary, the angels, and the saints signify Christ who is glorified in them (C 1145-1162).

The Church commemorates the mysteries of Christ's life in the liturgical year. Christ's Resurrection is celebrated each Sunday and especially at Easter, the greatest feast. The Church honors Mary and the saints as examples of faith and holiness (C 1163-1173).

The Liturgy of the Hours recalls Christ's saving mysteries and sanctifies the course of each day. Priests, religious, and laity are invited to say this prayer with devotion and with a proper understanding of the Bible, especially the Psalms (C 1174-1178).

Christian worship is not centered on any one place, but on the person of Jesus Christ. Christians are themselves temples of God's presence, but they build churches as places of worship and as signs that make the Church visible. A church building should be constructed in good taste. The altar symbolizes the cross of Christ and is the table of the Lord. The tabernacle should be situated in a most fitting place with the greatest honor. Other elements that deserve special attention are sacred chrism and blessed oils, the bishop's or priest's chair, the lectern, the baptismal font, and a place appropriate for celebrating the sacrament of Penance. The church building should encourage prayer and recollection. Entering a church foreshadows our entry into everlasting life (C 1179-1199).

Liturgical Diversity, One Mystery

Christ's paschal mystery has been celebrated through the centuries in many cultures and traditions. The approved rites in the Catholic Church—Latin, Byzantine, Alexandrian or Coptic, Syriac, Armenian, Maronite, and Chaldean—are of equal dignity and should be preserved. The mystery of Christ should be proclaimed to all nations in a manner which redeems and fulfills the culture of each. That part of the liturgy which was divinely instituted by Christ is unchangeable, but other parts can be adapted in ways faithful to apostolic Tradition (C 1200-1209).

The Seven Sacraments

Christ instituted seven sacraments which touch all the stages of Christian life. They are divided into three categories: initiation (Baptism, Confirmation, and Eucharist), healing (Penance and Anointing of the Sick), and service (Holy Orders and Matrimony). The sacraments of initiation lay the foundation for Christian life. Baptism gives new life which is then strengthened by Confirmation and nourished by the Eucharist (C 1210-1212).

Baptism

Baptism is our entry into Christian life. *Baptism* comes from the Greek *baptizein*, meaning "to immerse" or "to plunge" into water. It symbolizes our participation in Christ's death and Resurrection. Being immersed or washed in water signifies the removal (the "death") of sin. Rising from the water symbolizes our rising to the new life of grace (C 1213-1216).

Baptism is foreshadowed in the Old Testament. At Creation the Spirit breathed life onto the waters, and the Spirit gives new life through the water of Baptism.

Noah's ark saved humanity and brought a new beginning, as does Baptism. The Exodus and crossing of the Red Sea liberated the Israelites from slavery, as Baptism liberates us from sin. The crossing of the Jordan symbolizes our entry through Baptism into the Promised Land of heaven (C 1217-1222).

These Old Covenant symbols are fulfilled in Christ, whose baptism by John in the Jordan prefigured the sacrament Christ established when he sent his apostles to teach and baptize. Jesus spoke of his Passion as a baptism (Luke 12:50). The water and blood flowing from his side as he died on the cross are signs of Baptism and the Eucharist. Beginning on Pentecost, the apostles taught the necessity of Baptism and its connection with faith, for Baptism joins the believer to Christ's death and Resurrection (C 1223-1228).

Baptism includes several stages which may be covered in different ways, but the sacrament always involves proclamation of the Word, acceptance of the Gospel, profession of faith, Baptism itself, the outpouring of the Holy Spirit, and admission to the Eucharist. Those baptized in infancy go through some of these stages in a postbaptismal catechesis. Since Vatican II, adults who are baptized are received into the Church through the *Rite of Christian Initiation of Adults (RCIA)* (C 1229-1233).

The actual celebration of Baptism begins with the sign of the cross, a reminder that Christ redeemed us by his cross. God's Word is proclaimed to elicit a response of faith. Exorcisms are pronounced to express our liberation from sin and the devil. The candidate is anointed with the oil of catechumens and renounces Satan. Water is blessed. The minister confers Baptism by immersing the candidate three times or by pouring water over the candidate's head three times, while saying: "N., I baptize you in the name of the Father, and of the Son, and of the Holy Spirit." The newly baptized is anointed with sacred chrism (perfumed oil), signifying the bestowal of the Holy Spirit. A white garment is placed on the newly baptized, an action which symbolizes being clothed with Christ. A candle, lit from the Easter candle, represents the enlightenment given by Christ. The newly baptized is now a child of God who can pray "Our Father" with Jesus and can receive Jesus in Holy Communion. The ceremony closes with a blessing (C 1234-1245).

Anyone not baptized is eligible for Baptism. Adults are first prepared through the catechumenate, which should be a formation in Christian life involving instruction, formation, and introduction into God's people by successive sacred rites. Those in the catechumenate are already members of the Church (C 1246-1249).

Infant Baptism may have originated in New Testament times when whole households were baptized. Infant Baptism shows that grace is God's gift, not something earned. It frees children from original sin and welcomes them into God's kingdom. Parents should make this gift available to their children and then nurture God's life in them (C 1250-1252).

The beginnings of faith celebrated at Baptism must be nourished in the community of the Church. Adults are to grow in faith, as signified by the renewal of baptismal promises at every Easter Vigil. Infants need the help of parents and godparents, who must be firm believers (C 1253-1255).

The ordinary ministers of Baptism are the bishop, priest, or deacon. In case of necessity, anyone with the intention of doing what the Church does may baptize (C 1256).

Baptism is necessary for salvation for those who hear the Gospel and have an opportunity to receive this sacrament (John 3:5). Those who are martyred for Christ before they can be baptized are saved through Baptism of blood. Those who desire Baptism but die before receiving the sacrament also receive its benefits (Baptism of desire). Those who do not know Christ but seek the truth and strive to do God's will have an implicit desire for Baptism and can be saved. Children who die without Baptism are entrusted to God's mercy in the Church's funeral rites. God's compassion and Jesus' love for children allow us to hope that they can enter heaven (C 1257-1261).

Baptism brings forgiveness of all sins, original and personal, as well as freedom from any punishment due to sin. However, some consequences of sin remain, such as suffering, death, character weaknesses, and the inclination to sin (concupiscence). Baptism brings new life, making us children of God, sharers in the divine nature, and temples of the Holy Spirit. Through Baptism God confers sanctifying grace (the grace of justification), thus enabling us to believe, hope, and love; to be assisted by the gifts of the Holy Spirit; and to grow in goodness. Baptism joins us to the Church, the Body of Christ, giving us a share in the priesthood of believers. Baptism confers the obligation of serving the Church loyally, as well as the right to be ministered to by the Church. Baptism makes us one with all the baptized, including those who are not yet in full communion with the Catholic Church. Baptism bestows a character, an indelible spiritual mark signifying that we belong to Christ, that we are privileged to worship in the liturgy, and that we are destined to rise from death and live eternally with God (C 1262-1284).

Confirmation

Confirmation is necessary for the completion of baptismal grace, for it conveys the special strength of the Holy Spirit. Old Testament prophets announced that the Holy Spirit would rest upon the Messiah (Isaiah 11:2). Jesus was conceived by the Holy Spirit, and when he was baptized by John, the Spirit descended upon him. Christ gave the Holy Spirit to his followers on Easter and at Pentecost. They then baptized others and bestowed the Holy Spirit through the laying on of hands.

Both Baptism and the laying on of hands were fundamental elements of early Christian instruction (Hebrews 6:2). Soon an anointing with chrism was added. It highlighted the name *Christian* as denoting those who were anointed followers of Christ, the Anointed One (C 1285-1289).

In the East, Baptism, Confirmation, and Eucharist have always been bestowed together. In the West, Confirmation was separated from Baptism to allow the bishop to celebrate Confirmation. At the Baptism of infants, an anointing with chrism signifies the bestowal of the Holy Spirit and anticipates Confirmation (C 1290-1292).

Anointing with chrism at Confirmation signifies consecration to the mission of Christ and the Spirit's strength given for this mission. Confirmation is a seal that marks us as belonging to Christ as he belonged to the Father (2 Corinthians 1:21-22; John 6:27; C 1293-1296.)

Sacred chrism is blessed by the bishop at the Chrism Mass of Holy Thursday for use in the sacrament of Confirmation. When Confirmation is celebrated apart from Baptism, it begins with the renewal of baptismal promises that shows the connection of the two sacraments. The minister, with arms outstretched, says a prayer asking God to bestow the Holy Spirit. The essential rite of the sacrament involves the laying on of hands and the anointing with chrism while the minister says, "Be sealed with the Gift of the Holy Spirit." A sign of peace follows to signify union with the bishop and the Church (C 1297-1301).

Confirmation brings the full outpouring of the Holy Spirit as at Pentecost. It increases baptismal grace, joins us more closely to God and the Church, augments the gifts of the Spirit, and strengthens us to spread and defend the faith. Like Baptism, it imparts a character and may be received only once (C 1302-1305).

Every baptized person should receive Confirmation, for without it Baptism, though valid, remains incomplete. In the Latin tradition, the age of discretion is given as the proper time for Confirmation. When in danger of death, however, even young children should be confirmed. Ordinarily, preparation for Confirmation includes catechesis, prayer, and the sacrament of Penance. Candidates must be in a state of grace. They should have a sponsor, most appropriately a baptismal godparent (C 1306-1311).

The original minister of Confirmation is the bishop, though he may delegate priests for a grave reason. When adults are baptized or received into the Church by profession of faith, they are confirmed by the priest who receives them. When a Catholic, even a child, is in danger of death, any priest should administer Confirmation (C 1312-1321).

Eucharist

The Eucharist completes Christian initiation and is the source and summit of Christian life, for the sacrament *is* Christ. Eucharist unites us to God, to the community of believers, and to the Church in heaven. Its richness is expressed in the many names given it: Eucharist (thanksgiving), the Lord's Supper, the breaking of bread, the Eucharistic Assembly, the memorial of the Lord's Passion and Resurrection, the Holy Sacrifice, the Divine Liturgy, Holy Communion, Holy Mass (from *missio*, "sending forth") and many others (C 1322-1332).

In the Eucharist, bread and wine become Christ's body and blood. The Church sees the Eucharist prefigured in Melchizedek's offering of bread and wine (Genesis 14:18). Other Old Covenant foreshadowings include sacrificial offerings of bread and wine, manna in the desert, and the Passover meal's unleavened bread and cup of blessing. Jesus prefigured the Eucharist when he multiplied food for hungry crowds, and he first announced it at Capernaum (C 1333-1336).

Jesus instituted the Eucharist at the Last Supper, which he celebrated with his apostles on the Jewish feast of Passover. Taking bread, he told the apostles that it was his body. He took a cup of wine and pronounced it to be his blood. Jesus asked the apostles to do what he had done in remembrance of him, for he wanted his apostles and their successors to celebrate his Passion and Resurrection always. Christians obeyed him from the very beginning, as they met on Sunday to break bread (Acts of the Apostles 2:42; 20:7). The Church will continue to celebrate the Eucharist until Christ comes again (C 1337-1344).

A letter written by Saint Justin Martyr about A.D. 155 testifies that Christians followed the same basic pattern in celebrating the Eucharist as we do today. This pattern has two main parts: the Liturgy of the Word and the Liturgy of the Eucharist. The bishop or priest presides in the name of Christ who is the principal agent of the Eucharist; all others at the assembly participate in their own way. After prayers and Scripture readings, gifts of bread and wine are brought forth and offerings are given for the poor. The eucharistic prayer thanks God, asks for the blessing of the Spirit, repeats Jesus' words that change bread and wine into his body and blood, recalls Christ's Passion and Resurrection, and invokes heaven's assistance for the Church on earth. After the Lord's Prayer and the breaking of bread, the faithful receive Christ's body and blood (C 1345-1355).

We celebrate the Eucharist in the same substantive form as did the first believers because we believe that this form comes from Christ. We consider the Eucharist, as Jesus did, under three aspects: thanksgiving and praise, sacrificial memorial, and presence (C 1356-1358).

The Eucharist is *thanksgiving* and *praise*. We praise God for the beauty and goodness of creation, for redemption, and for sanctification. Eucharist means "thanksgiving," and we praise the Father through, with, and in Christ (C 1359-1361).

The Eucharist is a *sacrificial memorial*. At Mass we remember and proclaim Christ's sacrificial death and glorious Resurrection. The Eucharist makes present Christ's body given for us and his blood poured out for us. It makes present the sacrifice of the cross, remembering it and applying its graces to us. The Eucharist is the same sacrifice as that of the cross; only the manner of offering is different. Through the Eucharist, Christ's sacrifice becomes that of his Church, and its members can offer themselves to the Father in union with Christ. The whole Church—pope, bishop, priest, and community—prays with Christ and is joined to Mary and the saints in heaven. The Church intercedes for the departed who are not fully united with Christ so that they may enjoy eternal life in heaven (C 1362-1372).

The Eucharist is the *presence of Christ*. While Christ is present to the Church in many real ways, his presence in the Eucharist is unique. The substance of bread and wine becomes the substance of the body and blood of Christ in a change called *transubstantiation*. Only the appearances of bread and wine remain. The whole Christ is truly present where before there had been bread and wine. Christ's eucharistic presence begins at the words of consecration and lasts as long as the eucharistic species (appearances of bread and wine) subsist. He is present in any part of the species when the bread is broken or the wine poured. We worship the eucharistic Christ in many ways: genuflecting and bowing, adoring Jesus at Mass and outside Mass, exposing the host for veneration, and carrying it in procession. So that the Eucharist may be brought to the sick and be worshiped by the faithful, consecrated hosts are kept in a tabernacle, which should be located in an especially worthy place in the church. We should express our love and reverence for Christ in the Eucharist by adoring him with faith and devotion (C 1373-1381).

The Mass is both sacrificial memorial and sacred banquet, and the altar is both altar of sacrifice and table of the Lord. Christ invites us to come to the table to receive him in Holy Communion, but first we must prepare ourselves. Anyone conscious of grave sin (see page 74) must first receive the sacrament of Penance. We should all humbly express our unworthiness, as well as our realization that Christ can heal us. We should observe the fast required before Communion and show our reverence for Christ by our demeanor and clothing. Church law requires that we attend Mass on Sundays and holy days and that we receive the Eucharist at least once a year, if possible during the Easter season. We are encouraged to receive Communion every time we attend Mass, even daily. We receive the whole Christ under the species of bread or wine, but the sign of the eucharistic meal is more complete when Communion is given under both species (C 1382-1390).

Holy Communion brings many benefits. Communion strengthens our union with Christ (John 6:57). What food does for our physical body, Communion achieves for our spirit, giving us strength and enabling us to grow in the life of grace received at Baptism. Communion separates us from sin for it deepens our love, thus wiping away venial sins and preserving us from future mortal sins. Communion joins us more closely to one another in the Body of Christ, the Church, and helps us to recognize Christ in the poor (1 Corinthians 10:16-17). Intercommunion with Eastern churches that have apostolic succession is encouraged, given suitable circumstances and approval of Church authority. In churches which do not have the sacraments of Holy Orders and the Eucharist, intercommunion is not possible for Catholics. However, in cases of grave necessity Catholic ministers may give the sacraments of Eucharist, Penance, and Anointing of the Sick to other Christians not in full communion with the Church if they ask of their own accord, have the proper dispositions, and believe the Church's doctrine about these sacraments (C 1391-1401).

The Eucharist anticipates the heavenly glory promised us by Jesus. At the Last Supper, Jesus told his apostles that he would share the heavenly banquet with them. At Mass we look forward to seeing Christ face to face, and each Eucharist is a pledge of the life to come (C 1402-1419).

Living the Sacraments

At Mass Den held his two year-old-daughter, Mary Beth, who was a bit restless. As the priest lifted the host just before Holy Communion, Den directed Mary Beth's gaze toward the altar. "Look, Mary Beth," he whispered, "the priest is holding Jesus." Mary Beth looked intently at the priest, then replied, "That's not Jesus, Daddy. That's bread." Turning to Den, she pinched his cheek and asked, "Daddy, do you need glasses?"

No, Daddy doesn't need glasses, and soon Mary Beth will see Jesus, too, with the eyes of faith. Faith gives us the vision to see Jesus in the Eucharist and in every act of the liturgy.

Eyes of faith and the Church's teaching about liturgy and sacraments can expand our horizons. Every act of worship is an invitation to meet our Creator. Our Baptism bestowed gifts which are ours today: God's own life; the presence of Father, Son, and Spirit within us; the grace to follow Jesus; the insight that God is available in all creation. Confirmation strengthened us to make the most of each day, to live by the Spirit—with love, courage, and hope. The Eucharist unites us to Jesus now and promises that we shall live forever. "Yes, Mary Beth. The bread has become Jesus, and he loves us all. We see him, we meet him, in the liturgy and sacraments."

Questions for Discussion or Reflection

The *Catechism* states that at the liturgy we gather to worship God, proclaim the Gospel, and serve our neighbor. How do we accomplish each of these actions at Sunday Mass?

We need eyes of faith to see the mysteries involved in each sacrament. What do you see with eyes of faith at Baptism, Confirmation, and Eucharist? What do those without faith see? Which is the reality?

Activities

Picture yourself receiving Baptism, with Jesus himself pouring the water over your head. Envision yourself being confirmed, seeing Jesus place his hands on your head, sending the Holy Spirit upon you. See yourself receiving Holy Communion from Jesus himself, as the apostles did at the Last Supper. Thank Jesus because this is the reality...for you and for anyone who receives the sacraments!

Chapter Eight

SACRAMENTS OF
HEALING AND SERVICE

A woman went to the doctor's office to have her blood pressure checked. First to arrive, she sat waiting so long that her leg fell asleep. When the nurse finally called her, the woman limped painfully into the examination room. A few minutes later, she walked briskly through the waiting room and out the door. Two other patients stared in disbelief. One nudged the other and said, "What did I tell you? He's the best doctor in town."

Perhaps! But there is no doubt that Christ is the best physician of all. He healed broken bodies and restored life to afflicted spirits. He continues these ministries in the Church through the sacraments of healing—Penance and Anointing of the Sick (C 1420-1421).

Penance

The sacrament of Penance—also called the sacrament of conversion, of confession, of forgiveness, of Reconciliation—bestows God's pardon on repentant sinners and reconciles them with the Church. It gives us the opportunity to admit our sins, grants God's forgiveness, and reunites us with God and neighbor (C 1422-1424).

Baptism takes away sin and gives us Christ's life, but it does not remove our inclination to sin. Even after the first conversion of Baptism, we fail and must continually strive for conversion from sin (C 1425-1429).

Jesus calls us to an interior conversion of heart. This conversion includes aversion for sin, determination to change, hope in God's mercy, and sorrow for our failings. It finds expression in fasting, prayer, almsgiving, making peace, concern for the salvation of others, intercession of the saints, and the practice of charity. Conversion is accomplished by gestures of reconciliation, care for the poor, works of justice, examination of conscience, acceptance of suffering, and especially by taking up the cross each day in imitation of Jesus. Conversion is nourished by the Eucharist, Scripture, prayer, and liturgical seasons of penance (C 1430-1439).

Sin offends God and damages our communion with the Church. Therefore, reconciliation with God necessitates reconciliation with the Church. Only God can forgive sins, but Christ gave his apostles and their successors the power to absolve sins in his name and to welcome sinners back to the eucharistic table (John 20:19-23). At first this power was exercised through penitential rites that included prolonged public penance by those who had sinned grievously. By the seventh century the sacrament employed a private rite for lesser as well as for mortal sins, a form retained to the present day. The sacrament always includes contrition, confession, and satisfaction on the part of the sinner, culminating in God's forgiveness through absolution: "I absolve you from your sins" (C 1440-1449).

Contrition is the first requirement for a penitent. Sorrow which arises from love of God is called *perfect* contrition; it remits even mortal sins if the penitent has the intention of receiving the sacrament of Penance as soon as possible. *Imperfect* contrition is sorrow emanating from fear of damnation or repugnance for sin; it disposes the sinner to receive forgiveness in the sacrament of Penance. *Confession*, the second requirement, should be preceded by an examination of conscience. Confessing our sins helps us face and conquer them. Confession of all mortal sins is necessary for forgiveness and is required by Church law at least once a year or anytime before receiving Communion. Confession of venial sins is not strictly necessary but is recommended for its many spiritual benefits. *Satisfaction*, the third requirement, is the act of reparation for any harm done by sin. The penance imposed by the confessor is a part of this reparation and should be directed to meet the penitent's spiritual needs (C 1450-1460).

The ministers of this sacrament are bishops and priests. They bestow God's forgiveness through the prayer of *absolution*. They continue the ministry of Christ, the Good Shepherd, and should serve as signs of God's merciful love with competence, compassion, and patience. They are bound to absolute secrecy (the sacramental seal) regarding sins told in confession (C 1461-1467).

This sacrament brings reconciliation with God and the Church, peace of soul, and spiritual consolation. Penance anticipates our judgment at death and opens us to eternal life (C 1468-1470).

Closely linked to the effects of Penance are indulgences. An indulgence is the Church's declaration that prayers or actions have special value because they share in the grace of Christ and in the good works of the saints, the spiritual treasury of the Church. Indulgences and other penitential practices can help us attain complete purification from sin and the temporal punishment due to sin. Indulgences may also be obtained for the faithful departed who are being purified, for they, too, are members of the communion of saints (C 1471-1479).

The sacrament of Penance ordinarily includes a greeting and blessing from the priest, Scripture, confession, the assigning of a penance, absolution, prayer of praise, and dismissal. The sacrament may be administered within the framework of a communal celebration with individual confessions. In case of grave necessity, there may be a communal celebration with general confession and absolution, but those in serious sin must intend to confess their sins individually as soon as possible. Personal confession allows Christ to meet each sinner and is the ordinary means of reconciliation with the Church (C 1480-1498).

Anointing of the Sick

Sickness and suffering can either drag us down to despair or lift us up to God. Old Testament hopes for victory over suffering were fulfilled when Christ entered the world. He healed the sick and took upon himself the world's suffering in his Passion. He gave the Church a share in his ministry of compassion and healing, and the Church has responded by caring for the sick and by recognizing, in James 5:14-15, the Lord's design for the sacrament of the Anointing of the Sick. The Church teaches that this sacrament is for the seriously ill. They are to be anointed with oil on the forehead and hands while the minister says the appropriate prayer (C 1499-1513).

Anyone who begins to be in danger of death from sickness or old age may receive the anointing, and it may be repeated if the illness grows worse or returns. Bishops and priests are the proper ministers of this sacrament. The anointing may be administered in conjunction with the Eucharist. Its effects include the grace of spiritual strength in the face of suffering—a gift of the Holy Spirit—as well as physical healing if this is God's will. Those unable to confess their sins are forgiven. The sick are united to Christ's Passion and are helped to offer their suffering as a prayer for others. They are prepared for entry into everlasting life. For the dying, the anointing may be ministered in a continuous rite with Penance and Communion (C 1514-1532).

Sacraments of Service

Father Wendelin Dunker, a retired missionary, was invited to say grace at a family Christmas dinner. He rose and blessed the meal, using a spontaneous prayer instead of the usual "Bless us, O Lord, and these thy gifts...." He noticed that the smaller children, seated at a little table nearby, seemed to be shaking their heads as if to say, "That's not how you say grace." Father Dunker was invited to the same home on the following Christmas and once again blessed the meal in his own words. As he sat down, he heard a little boy whisper loudly to another, "He still hasn't learned it!"

Christ, the priest, blessed a special family celebration at Cana. Priests and families have been connected in many ways ever since. The sacraments of service that commission people to carry out priestly ministry and establish families, Holy Orders and Matrimony, are directed toward Christlike service of others (C 1533-1535).

Holy Orders

Holy Orders is the sacrament through which Christ continues the ministry he entrusted to his apostles. It includes three degrees: episcopacy (bishops), presbyterate (priests), and diaconate (deacons). *Ordination* means being incorporated into one of the ranks of Holy Orders. This sacrament confers a gift of the Holy Spirit allowing the one ordained to exercise sacred power (C 1536-1538).

The priesthood of Aaron and Levi and that of the priest-king Melchizedek prefigured the unique priesthood of Christ. Only Christ's redemptive sacrifice of the cross could save humankind. This sacrifice is made present in the Eucharist, and Christ's priesthood is made present in the sacrament of Holy Orders. Christ's presence guarantees that his grace will always be available in the sacraments, but it does not remove the weaknesses of the ministers. Priests are human beings capable of sin; they are nevertheless called to serve faithfully in the name of Christ and the Church (C 1539-1553).

The Church recognizes the episcopacy and presbyterate as the two degrees of ministerial participation in Christ's priesthood. The diaconate is a ministry of service designed to help the other two. All three are conferred by the sacrament of Holy Orders (C 1554).

Bishops receive the fullness of the sacrament. Episcopal consecration confers the offices of teaching, ruling, and sanctifying, as well as a permanent sacred character empowering bishops to act as representatives of Christ. Bishops are ordained by other bishops, and lawful ordination requires the pope's intervention. Bishops care for the local church entrusted to them and, with other bishops, serve the whole Church (C 1555-1561).

Priests are anointed with the Spirit and signed with a character to act in the person of Christ. They depend on their bishops in the exercise of priestly ministry as they preach the Gospel, shepherd the faithful, and celebrate liturgy. They fulfill their office in the highest degree at the Eucharist. Priests represent their bishop to the faithful and, under the bishop, form one priestly body (C 1562-1568).

Deacons are marked by ordination with a character giving them a special likeness to Christ as servant of all. Deacons assist priests and bishops in liturgical celebrations, baptize (see C 1256), distribute Holy Communion, bless marriages, proclaim the Gospel, preach, preside at funerals, and perform works of charity. The diaconate may be conferred on married men (C 1569-1571).

Ordinations should take place in the presence of the faithful. The essential rite for all three orders consists in the imposition of hands and the consecratory prayer by the bishop. Only baptized men may validly receive ordination, and they must be called by God through the Church. Bishops and priests in the Latin Church are chosen from men of faith who intend to remain celibate for the sake of God's kingdom (Matthew 19:12). The sacrament of Holy Orders configures the ordinand to Christ for service as his representative. Because it confers a permanent character, it cannot be repeated or administered temporarily (C 1572-1600).

Matrimony

Marriage is God's design for humanity and a mystery mirroring Christ's love for the Church. Sin has marred the institution of marriage, so men and women must turn to God for grace to overcome sin and to achieve loving unity (C 1601-1608).

After the Fall of Adam and Eve, marriage was a constant invitation to generosity and service. But God's design for marriage was recognized only gradually in the Old Covenant and was fully realized when Christ elevated marriage to a new level. Jesus worked his first miracle at the wedding feast of Cana, proclaimed the unity and indissolubility of marriage, offered married couples an example of sacrificial love, and raised marriage to the dignity of a sacrament (C 1609-1617).

Christ invites some men and women to sacrifice the good of marriage that they may follow him in the path of consecrated virginity. This state demonstrates that Christ is the center of Christian life, allows people to dedicate themselves in a special way to the service of God's kingdom, and shows that this world is passing away. Both the sacrament of Matrimony and the gift of consecrated virginity come from Jesus, and both are to be esteemed, for they reinforce each other (C 1618-1620).

Marriage between two Catholics should ordinarily be celebrated at Mass, and the couple should prepare for the celebration of marriage by receiving the sacrament of Penance. In the Latin Church, the spouses are the ministers of Matrimony. The priest or deacon who assists at a marriage receives the consent of the couple in the name of the Church and gives the blessing of the Church. His presence and that of the official witnesses show the connection between marriage and the Church. That matrimonial consent might be properly given, the spouses should prepare for marriage. Family and the Church have important roles in this preparation and in the sharing of human and Christian values of marriage. For matrimonial consent to be valid, it must be free of coercion or grave external fear and not forbidden by law. If freedom is lacking, the marriage is invalid. For this and other reasons the Church can declare the nullity of a marriage, meaning that a valid marriage never existed. Such declarations are commonly called annulments (C 1621-1632).

Special attention should be given to mixed marriages between Catholics and non-Catholics, where differences of belief can cause problems. Both parties need to be aware of the nature of marriage and of the Catholic's responsibility for the Catholic upbringing of children. The Catholic must obtain the required permission or dispensation from the bishop. While there are difficulties to be faced in a marriage between a Catholic and a nonbelieving spouse, the Catholic has an opportunity by good example and love to lead the spouse to conversion (C 1633-1637).

A valid marriage has for its first effect a permanent and exclusive bond uniting the spouses to each other and to God. Matrimony also bestows the grace needed to carry out the responsibilities of married life. Marriage brings with it the obligations of unity, faithfulness and indissolubility, and openness to fertility. Unity is strengthened by faith in Christ and by the Eucharist received together. Fidelity and indissolubility (permanence) are required by the very nature of marriage, by genuine love, and by the need to promote the good of children. In situations where couples separate or divorce after a valid marriage, a second civil marriage cannot be recognized by the Church. Those who contract a civil marriage after divorce may not receive Holy Communion. Pastors and others, however, should show solicitude toward such persons so that they do not consider themselves separated from the Church, but instead participate in the Church's life as baptized believers. Openness to fertility means following God's design and cooperating with God in bringing new life into the world (C 1638-1653).

Every family should form a domestic church, where parents teach their children the ways of faith. Spouses who cannot have children may still enjoy a conjugal life full of meaning and love. People who remain single should always find a welcome in the family of the Church (C 1654-1666).

Sacramentals

Sacramentals are sacred signs that resemble the seven sacraments. Instituted by the Church, they signify spiritual effects which come about primarily through the prayer of the Church. They demonstrate the Church's belief that material things can be directed to our sanctification and to the glory of God. Sacramentals do not bestow grace as the sacraments do, but they dispose us to receive the grace of the sacraments and sanctify various occasions in human life. Sacramental blessings may be said over people, places, and things, demonstrating that material creation is directed to our sanctification and God's glory. Many such blessings may be given by laypeople (C 1667-1673).

Popular Piety

Catholic piety finds expression in popular devotions, such as the veneration of relics, pilgrimages, the Stations of the Cross, the rosary, and medals. These devotions extend the liturgical life of the Church but do not replace it. They should always be in harmony with the liturgy and lead people to it. Popular piety expresses the wisdom and beliefs of various cultures and ought to be clarified and fostered in the light of faith (C 1674-1679).

Christian Funerals

Death is our passover into new life with Christ. The Church places deceased Christians in God's hands and commits their bodies to the earth. While Christian funerals do not confer any sacrament or sacramental on the deceased, who have passed beyond the sacramental realm, they are liturgical celebrations. The Eucharist, which may be celebrated for the deceased, is a sacrament, and the blessings before and after Mass are sacramentals which ask God's mercy for the departed. Funeral rites express our communion with the deceased, our ability to help them by our prayers, and our hope for eternal life. They include four principal elements. The *greeting of the community* offers the Spirit's consolation and the promise of everlasting life. The *Liturgy of the Word* illumines the mystery of Christian death. The *Eucharist* seeks God's pardon and grace for the deceased and expresses our communion with them. The *farewell* is the Church's final commendation of the deceased to God (C 1680-1690).

Christ's ministries of healing and service continue in the sacraments of Penance, Anointing of the Sick, Holy Orders, and Matrimony. In all the sacraments, Christ touches us with God's grace and love.

Questions for Discussion or Reflection

Christ gave confession of sins to the Church as the way to meet him in the sacrament of Penance. He could have chosen other ways. Why do you think he chose confession?

Many people mistakenly believe that suffering is always punishment for personal sin. How does the Anointing of the Sick, a sacrament which unites us to the suffering and death of Christ, show that this is not so?

What can you do to promote more vocations to the priesthood?

Describe the marriages that seem to really reflect Christ's love. What are your favorite sacramentals and devotions?

Activities

Consider the vocation to which you have been called by God. Thank God for this vocation and for the opportunities you have to be of service to others. Jesus said that we should pray for workers in God's vineyard. Pray that more people may respond to Christ's call to serve him in the priesthood, religious life, marriage, and the single state.

Part Three

Life
in Christ

Chapter Nine

LIFE IN CHRIST

A class of second-graders was asked by their religion teacher, "What is conscience?" A little girl raised her hand and said, "Conscience is the voice that tells you to stop when you are beating up your little brother. My conscience has saved him many times." Even second-graders know right from wrong!

The Creed teaches that we are created as God's children, given new life by Christ, and made holy by the Spirit. The sacraments communicate the Father's love, the grace of Christ, and the gifts of the Spirit. Instructed by the Creed and blessed by the sacraments, we are called to live as Christ teaches, to do good and avoid evil. Christ's way leads to life. The contrary way leads to death. We learn Christ's way in a catechesis that teaches the Holy Spirit, grace, the beatitudes, the reality of sin and forgiveness, human and Christian virtues, love of God and neighbor—a catechesis that is ecclesial and Christ-centered (C 1691-1698).

Made in God's Image

Life in the Spirit is our vocation. We are created in God's image and likeness, especially in that God has given us intellect and will. Our intellect allows us to understand God's command to do good and avoid evil. Our will lets us freely choose to obey the moral law heard in our conscience. Original sin inclines us to evil, but Christ gives us strength to conquer sin. Faith in him makes us God's children and enables us to live in the perfection of charity and attain eternal life in heaven (C 1699-1715).

Beatitude and the Beatitudes

We are made for beatitude, for happiness. The Eight Beatitudes teach us Christ's way to the happiness that is supernatural and made possible by God's grace (Matthew 5:3-12). They present attitudes which shape our conduct after the pattern set by Jesus. They promise the joy of seeing God forever in heaven. Since we have been made to know, love, and serve God, true happiness can be found in God alone, not in riches, fame, or power. We must, therefore, love God above all else and make moral choices that lead us to God (C 1716-1729).

Human Freedom

God made us rational and free. Freedom is the power, rooted in reason and will, to perform deliberate actions for which we are responsible. Freedom allows us to choose between good and evil. It characterizes properly human acts and is the basis of praise or blame. Doing good makes us truly free, while doing evil makes us slaves of sin. Because freedom is God's gift, we are responsible for our acts to the extent that they are voluntary, either directly or indirectly, as when someone out of culpable (deserving blame) ignorance causes a traffic accident. Freedom and responsibility, however, can be diminished or nullified by ignorance, force, fear, habit, and other factors. Every human being has the right to exercise freedom, and this right, especially in moral and religious matters, must be respected. But freedom does not mean the license to do or say everything, right or wrong. Moreover, the proper exercise of freedom is sometimes impeded by human sinfulness or by economic, social, political, and cultural conditions. Christ has redeemed us from the bonds of sin, and his grace enables us to use our freedom to choose what is true and good (C 1730-1748).

The Morality of Human Acts

Human acts are morally good or evil depending on their object, intention, and circumstances. The *object* is what a person chooses, for example, a good act, such as almsgiving, or an evil one, such as theft. The *intention* is the act of the will, one's purpose in choosing an object. A bad intention can vitiate (negate, invalidate) even a good act, as when a person gives alms to win praise. A good intention, however, cannot justify something which is evil in itself. *Circumstances* are secondary elements of a moral act and contribute to the goodness or evil of that act. The amount taken in a theft, for example, helps determine the degree of sinfulness; fear or coercion can diminish culpability. Object, intention, and circumstances determine the morality of human acts, and all three must be good for an action to be good (C 1749-1761).

The Passions

In traditional theology, passions refer to emotions or feelings, movements of our sensitive appetite that incline us to act or to refrain from acting. Among these passions are love and hatred, desire and fear, sadness and anger. Such emotions are neither good nor evil in themselves. Moral qualifications derive from the extent that the emotions are governed by reason and will. Passions become morally good when they contribute to a good action, evil when they contribute to an evil action. Thus, Jesus' anger was good because it helped motivate him to drive merchants from the Temple. Cain's anger was evil because it drove him to murder his brother, Abel. Strong feelings are not necessary for morality or holiness, but in the Christian life our passions and emotions, mobilized by the Holy Spirit, can attract us to God and to moral goodness (C 1762-1775).

Conscience

Conscience is a judgment of reason whereby we recognize the goodness or evil of an action. Conscience is sometimes portrayed as a voice telling us right from wrong or as a law written in our hearts. Through conscience, God disposes us to good and turns us from evil, and so we must attend to it. Conscience includes the perception of the principles of morality, their application in given circumstances, and judgment with regard to particular acts. Conscience enables us to assume responsibility for our actions, and when we do evil, conscience calls us to repentance. Conscience must be properly formed through education based on God's Word, assisted by the Holy Spirit, supported by the counsel of others, and guided by the Church's teaching (C 1776-1785).

Faced with moral choices, conscience can make a right or a wrong judgment. At times, making a proper judgment is difficult, but we must always strive to seek what is right according to God's will. In this we are helped by the virtue of prudence, the advice of wise counselors, the guidance of the Holy Spirit, and clear norms such as the golden rule. We must always obey the certain judgment of conscience, but it is possible for conscience to make uninformed judgments. When ignorance or error is the result of sinful neglect or slavery to passions, we are responsible. If we are not responsible for our ignorance, then culpability cannot be attributed to us, but we must always strive to overcome error and be guided by objective standards of moral conduct (C 1786-1802).

Virtues

Virtues are good habits that help us to do the right thing. *Human virtues* are those which govern our actions, regulate our passions, and guide our conduct according to reason and faith. They help us live a good life more easily and joyfully. Four of them are so significant that they are called the cardinal virtues (from the Latin word for *hinge*, because so many other virtues hinge on them). *Prudence* helps us discern the right thing to do in any circumstance and guides our conscience in making judgments. *Justice* enables us to give God and others their due. *Fortitude* strengthens us to do good, to weather the difficulties and temptations of life, and to overcome fear. *Temperance* helps us control our desires and use the good things of life in a Christlike way. These and other virtues are acquired by study and persevering effort aided by God's grace obtained especially through prayer and the sacraments (C 1803-1811).

The *theological virtues* are so named because they are gifts of God and direct our relationship to God. By *faith* we believe in God and accept the truths that God reveals. We express our faith by good works, by professing it, and by spreading it. By *hope* we desire heaven as our final goal and have confident assurance of achieving it with the help of God's grace. Hope keeps us from despair and self-centeredness and leads us to the happiness that comes from charity. Hope is proclaimed in Christ's teaching, sustained by his merits, and nourished at prayer. By *charity* we love God above all and our neighbor as ourselves. Christian charity is modeled on the love of Jesus and strengthens us to keep the commandments. Charity, the greatest of the virtues, makes us God's children and helps us relate to others in joy, mercy, and peace (C 1812-1829).

Our efforts to practice virtue are sustained by the *gifts of the Holy Spirit*. These are wisdom, understanding, counsel, fortitude, knowledge, piety, and fear of the Lord (Isaiah 11:2). The Spirit's love within us produces the *fruits of the Holy Spirit*. They are charity, joy, peace, patience, kindness, goodness, generosity, gentleness, faithfulness, modesty, self-control, and chastity (Galatians 5:22-23). The gifts and fruits of the Spirit help us to lead Christlike lives (C 1830-1845).

Sin

When we acknowledge our sinfulness, we open ourselves to the mercy of God. Sin is disobedience to God's law, rejection of God's love, and preference of ourselves over God and neighbor. The evil done by sin is most evident in the Lord's Passion, at the very moment Christ was about to conquer the power of sin. Scripture lists many kinds of sins, and sin may be classified in many ways, but every sin is rooted in the misuse of freedom and the choice of evil over good (Galatians 5:19-21; C 1846-1853).

Sins are evaluated in terms of their gravity. *Mortal (grave) sins* are those which are so serious that they destroy love within us and turn us away from God, our final goal. For a sin to be mortal, three conditions must be present. First, there must be *grave matter*, something that causes significant harm to others or ourselves or is a serious affront to God (for example, murder, adultery, blasphemy). Second, there must be *full knowledge*; the sinner must be entirely aware of the wickedness of the action. Third, there must be *complete consent of the will*; the sinner must freely choose to do what is evil. Mental deficiency, unintentional ignorance, passion, and external forces can diminish the gravity of sin. But when grave matter, full knowledge, and complete consent are present, mortal sin exists and can cause eternal death for those who do not repent. Refusal to repent is that sin against the Holy Spirit for which Jesus says there is no forgiveness; impenitence by its nature rejects God's mercy. *Venial sins* are failings which do not destroy love or sever our bond of love with God. They involve less serious matter (such as theft of a small item), lack of full knowledge, or incomplete consent. Venial sin can weaken our friendship with God and lead to more serious failings, so we should try to overcome it with the help of God's grace (C 1854-1864).

Each act of sin inclines us to sin again. Tendencies to sin are called *vices*, which stand in contrast to the virtues they undermine. Vices are often associated with the *capital sins* of pride, avarice, envy, wrath, lust, gluttony, and sloth. Though sin is personal, it often involves cooperation with others and produces evil social structures and institutions that in turn cause sins to multiply. In contrast, good social structures promote true human values (C 1865-1876).

The Human Community

Another expression of our creation in God's image and likeness is human community. Just as God is a community of Persons, so we are created as persons who need community and society. A *society* is a group of persons bound together by a principle of unity that goes beyond each of them. Through society, people receive benefits from their ancestors and pass them on in turn to future generations. Some societies, such as the family and the state, flow from human nature and are necessary for survival. Other societies relating to economic, social, cultural, recreational, and political goals arise from the natural tendency to form mutually beneficial associations. All social institutions ought to exist for the sake of individual persons, and they should follow the *principle of subsidiarity*. This principle states that what can be done by a smaller body should not be usurped by a larger one and that larger societal groups should support smaller ones as they work for the common good. Just as God shares power with creatures, so leaders must share their authority. The principle of subsidiarity rules out collectivism, sets limits on state intervention, harmonizes relationships, and tends toward true international order. Societies must respect higher spiritual values, avoid turning means into ends, and appeal for conversion of heart so that all may follow the path of charity toward the establishment of justice. This can be accomplished only with the help of God's grace (C 1877-1896).

Society needs legitimate authority to maintain order, promote the common good, enact and enforce just laws. The fact that authority comes from God demands obedience to and respect for those in authority. The same fact requires that political leaders be chosen by citizens. Diverse political regimes are acceptable as long as they serve the good of the communities they govern. For authority to be legitimate, it must seek the common good, and there should be a balance of power that keeps authority within proper limits (C 1897-1904).

The *common good* is the sum total of social conditions that allow people as individuals and as groups to achieve fulfillment. It consists of three elements: respect for the fundamental rights of the human person; development of the spiritual and material well-being of society; and the establishment of peace, justice, and security. The state's role is to promote the common good of all. Increasing human interdependence calls for a community of nations able to advance the common good of humanity, always placing the good of individuals before that of the state. At every level of society, participation on the part of its members is necessary. People must take charge of areas for which they have personal responsibility, such as their families and occupations. They should participate in public life so that harmful influences might be eradicated and beneficial social structures might be enhanced (C 1905-1927).

Social Justice

Society brings about social justice by providing the conditions which allow individuals and associations to obtain what is rightfully theirs. Social justice depends upon respect for the dignity of each person and for God-given rights. Respect for the person flows from the principle that each one must consider the neighbor as another self. Christ's teaching urges us to pay particular heed to the disadvantaged and to show love to all, even enemies (C 1928-1933).

Because human beings have the same nature, origin, destiny, and dignity, every form of unjust discrimination ought to be eliminated. While people have the same human nature, they have different talents and abilities. They must work together generously to help one another, to eradicate sinful inequalities, and to promote human solidarity. Solidarity entails the just distribution of goods, fair pay for services, and peaceful striving for a just social order at every level of society. Solidarity includes the sharing of spiritual as well as material goods, and the Church shares the goods of the faith for the spiritual and temporal welfare of all (C 1934-1948).

At every level of human existence, from second-graders and their little broth-ers to the United Nations, we are called by God to distinguish good from evil, to see every person as a child of God, and to build societies that promote the justice and peace of God's kingdom.

Questions for Discussion or Reflection

Who is more free, those who follow God's law or those who do not? Why?

Can you explain in your own words what is meant by the object, intention, and circum-stances of human acts?

What virtues do you most admire in others? What sins or vices seem to be doing most harm in our society?

How is the Church working for social justice in the world? in the United States? in your parish?

In the *Catechism*, "mortal sin" and "grave sin" have the same meaning. Study the following paragraphs: 1385, 1446-47, 1453, 1470, 1472, 1493, 1497, 1861-62, 2120, 2181, and 2390. How are "mortal sin" and "grave sin" used interchangeably in these paragraphs?

Activities

Read Matthew 5:3-12, the beatitudes. Reflect on them as Jesus' way to happiness, especially in the light of what you have studied in this chapter. Ask God to help you, and all people, find happiness by following Christ.

Chapter Ten

LAW, GRACE, COMMANDMENTS, AND LOVE OF GOD

"Miracle drugs are fine," the pastor told his congregation, "but God gave Moses two tablets that can cure the world's ills."

Truer words were never spoken. The *Catechism* teaches the beauty of God's law and shows how we can keep that law with the help of God's grace. It reflects on the laws God has revealed, especially the Ten Commandments—laws written on two stone tablets and given to the world through Moses.

The Moral Law

We have been created for eternal happiness, but we need God's salvation to achieve it. So God offers grace to sustain us and law to guide us. *Law* may be defined as a rule of conduct passed by competent authority for the sake of the common good. *Moral law* points out actions which lead to eternal happiness and prohibits evil deeds which separate us from God. It finds expression in God's eternal law, in the natural law, in revealed law, and in civil and ecclesiastical laws (C 1949-1953).

Natural law is written on the soul of every person, enabling us to discern good from evil, right from wrong. Natural law states the most basic precepts governing the moral life. It is the light of understanding placed in us by God, showing us what we should do and what we should avoid. Its fundamental principles are common to all cultures and every age. It provides the foundation for upright living, human community, and civil law. But because its precepts are not easily perceived by everyone, God has revealed laws to direct us with clarity and certainty (C 1954-1960).

The laws of the Old Testament are the first stage of God's *revealed law*. They are summed up in the Ten Commandments and express many truths naturally accessible to reason. The Old Law is imperfect, pointing out obligations without offering the grace to fulfill them, but it prepared humanity for the Gospel (C 1961-1964).

The Law of the Gospel, the New Law, is the perfection of the divine law. It is Christ's work and is expressed primarily in the Sermon on the Mount. It is also the work of the Holy Spirit, through whom it becomes an interior law of love written on our hearts. It perfects the Old Law and fulfills the commandments by leading us to imitate the perfection of our heavenly Father. It is summed up in the golden rule and is contained in Jesus' command to love others as he has loved us. The New Law is further elaborated in apostolic teachings found in such passages as Romans 12-15, 1 Corinthians 12-13, Colossians 3-4, and Ephesians 4-5. It is a law of love because it helps us act out of love infused by the Holy Spirit. It is a law of grace because it bestows the strength to obey. It is a law of freedom because it guides us as friends of Christ rather than as servants. The New Law also includes the evangelical counsels (poverty, chastity, obedience), which remove obstacles to charity and help us reach the perfection of love (C 1965-1986).

Justification, Grace, Merit, and Holiness

Justification is the grace of the Holy Spirit that cleanses us from sin and communicates God's righteousness to us through faith in Christ and through Baptism. We are united to Christ's Passion by dying to sin. We are united to his Resurrection by rising to new life as members of his Body, the Church. The grace of the Holy Spirit first brings conversion, turning us from sin toward God and bringing about justification. Justification detaches us from sin and confers God's righteousness, empowering us to live in God's love. With justification come faith, hope, charity, and obedience to God's will. Justification was merited for us by Christ's Passion. It establishes cooperation between God's grace and our freedom; we can do nothing without God's grace, but we must freely cooperate with that grace. Justification leads to our sanctification as we follow the guidance of the Holy Spirit (C 1987-1995).

Justification comes from grace. *Grace* is God's favor, the free and undeserved help that makes us adoptive children of God, partakers of the divine nature, and heirs of heaven. Grace is a participation in the life of the Trinity; united with Jesus through Baptism, we can call God "Father" and receive the life of the Holy Spirit. This life is supernatural, beyond our human power. It is called *sanctifying grace* because it makes us holy. It is also called *habitual grace* because it is a permanent disposition to live God's life. It is distinguished from *actual graces*, God's special helps that prepare us for conversion or assist us as we follow Christ. God's free gift of grace demands our free response, for God does not force grace upon us. Among the graces God offers are *sacramental graces* conferred by the seven sacraments, the charisms which are *special graces* or gifts granted for the common good of the

Church, and *graces of state* which accompany responsibilities of Christian life and ministries within the Church. Because grace is supernatural, it can be perceived only by faith. We cannot know from feelings or our works that we are saved, but we can rely with confidence on God's mercy whose grace works in our lives (C 1996-2005).

Merit refers to the reward owed someone for a good act. Strictly speaking, we are owed nothing by God because all we have comes from God. But God has freely chosen to associate us with the work of grace. Any good deed results first from God's grace, then from our free collaboration with grace. Because we are adopted as God's children, God freely bestows true merit upon us, giving us the right to eternal life as a result of our cooperation with grace. We cannot merit the initial grace of justification, but assisted by the Holy Spirit, we can merit for ourselves and others the graces needed for sanctification and eternal life. We can also merit temporal goods like health, but with submission to God's wisdom and providence. And we must always remember that any merit of ours flows from the love of Christ (C 2006-2011).

Holiness is the perfection of charity; all are called to be perfect as our heavenly Father is perfect (Matthew 5:48). Growth in holiness tends toward intimate union with Christ. It always involves the cross and requires penance and mortification. As we strive for holiness, we trust in God for the grace of final perseverance and the joy of eternal life (C 2012-2029).

The Church, Mother and Teacher

It is in the Church that we learn God's law, receive God's grace, and are touched by the holiness of Mary and the saints. We offer our lives as spiritual worship in the Church's liturgy. The Church, "the pillar and bulwark of the truth" helps us live a moral life (1 Timothy 3:15). The magisterium, assisted by theologians and spiritual writers, hands down Catholic moral teaching and the basic tenets of the natural law. Those truths of faith and morals contained in divine Revelation and necessary for its preservation are guaranteed by the gift of infallibility. The faithful, for their part, have the right to be instructed in matters of morality and the duty to observe the Church's teachings. The Church needs the cooperation of believers in its work of teaching and applying Christian morality. Each should consider the good of all, and personal conscience should not be set in opposition to the moral law or magisterium of the Church (C 2030-2040).

The *precepts of the Church* are meant to establish the indispensable minimum for Christian moral life. These precepts command us to attend Mass and to rest from servile labor on Sundays and holy days of obligation, confess sins at least once a year, receive Holy Communion at least during the Easter season, observe days of fast and abstinence, and help provide for the material needs of the Church (C 2041-2043).

The faithful, by observing the moral precepts and teachings of the Church, proclaim to the world Christ's presence in the Church. They build up the Church and help bring about the completion of God's kingdom (C 2044-2051).

The Ten Commandments

When asked what must be done to attain eternal life, Jesus said, "Keep the commandments" (Matthew 19:17). Then Christ added a call to perfection, a call to observe the evangelical counsels. Jesus preached the Ten Commandments, and he also unveiled their full implications and their relationship to love of God and neighbor (C 2052-2055).

The Ten Commandments, also called the Decalogue ("ten words"), were given by God to Moses and are found in Exodus 20:1-17 and Deuteronomy 5:6-22. God granted them to people released from slavery, and the commandments show how to remain free of the slavery of sin. Revealed by God, they proclaim the righteousness of God and God's relationship to humanity through the Covenants. Since we are God's people, created and loved by God, addressed personally by God, we are to keep God's commandments. The Church has always acknowledged the importance of the commandments and presented them to the faithful in its catechisms. The traditional numbering of the commandments was established by Saint Augustine. (An alternate numbering was employed by the Greek churches and is followed in many Protestant denominations.) However they are counted, the commandments form a logical unity, teach us our fundamental responsibilities to God and others, and clearly proclaim some of the most basic requirements of natural law. Therefore, they reveal *grave* obligations that bind always and everywhere. They also involve obligations that are not grave in themselves, such as obedience in a light matter. We keep the Ten Commandments by depending upon union with Jesus and by following his mandate to love others as he loves us (C 2056-2082).

The First Commandment:

I am the Lord your God:
You shall not have strange gods before me.

God loves us, and Jesus teaches us to love God with our whole being. The first commandment bids us to express our love by adoration, by putting faith, hope, and love in God alone. *Faith* inspires us to believe God and to avoid the sins of voluntary doubt, incredulity, heresy (denial of a truth of faith), apostasy (total repudiation of faith), and schism (separating oneself from the Church's authority). *Hope* puts our reliance on God, giving us confidence in God's grace and promise of eternal life. It rules out the sins of despair (refusing to hope in God's mercy) and presumption (supposing either that we can save ourselves or that God will save us without effort on our part). *Charity* summons us to love God above all and to love others for God's sake. It forbids such sins as religious indifference, ingratitude, lukewarmness, spiritual sloth, and hatred of God (C 2083-2094).

This commandment orders us to give God what is due through the virtue of *religion*. The acts of this virtue include adoration (recognizing God as the Supreme Being and ourselves as creatures), prayer (lifting our minds and hearts to God), and sacrifice (uniting ourselves to Christ's sacrifice on the cross). Religion directs us to keep promises to God, especially those made at Baptism, Confirmation, Matrimony, and Holy Orders. It charges us to fulfill any vows made to God; of special importance are vows to keep the evangelical counsels of poverty, chastity, and obedience. Religion leads us to seek the truth found in the Catholic Church, always respecting people of different faiths. We are to evangelize the world, but no one may be forced to act against personal convictions in religious matters. Freedom from external constraint is a natural right which should be protected by civil law (C 2095-2109).

The first commandment forbids the worship of false gods and the sins of superstition, idolatry, divination, magic, irreligion, atheism, and agnosticism. *Superstition* attributes special powers to actions, objects, or mere external religious practices. *Idolatry* is the worship of pagan idols, demons, power, pleasure, money, ancestors, the state, or anything that is not God. *Divination* is the effort to learn the future through astrology, demons, horoscopes or any other supposed power. *Magic,* or sorcery, is the attempt to control occult powers to help oneself or to help or harm others. *Irreligion* includes the sins of tempting God (putting God's goodness to the test in some way), sacrilege (profaning anything sacred or anyone dedicated to God), and simony (buying or selling spiritual things). *Atheism* denies the reality of God and places ultimate value in material things, in humanity itself, or in economic and social development, perhaps in a misguided effort to exalt human dignity, which can only be truly recognized when God's place is acknowledged. *Agnosticism* proposes that God cannot be known and often ends up in religious indifference. Finally, the first commandment forbids the making of idolatrous images. It does not forbid all religious images, for the Old Testament commanded the creation of the bronze serpent, the Ark, and the cherubim. The Church encourages the veneration of icons of Christ, Mary, the angels, and the saints. These are not idols, but images which honor Christ and the saints while directing us to true worship of God alone (C 2110-2141).

The Second Commandment:

You shall not take the name of the Lord your God in vain.

God, by revealing the divine name to Moses, invited us to use that name with faith and reverence. The second commandment orders us to respect the name of God, using it only to praise and worship God. It mandates veneration for the names of Jesus Christ, of Mary, and of the saints. This commandment forbids blasphemy (words of hatred, reproach, or defiance against God), false oaths, perjury, and any other misuse of God's name. Oaths may be taken in court, but they must not be made for trivial or immoral purposes. Related to reverence for holy names is respect for the name Christians receive at Baptism. This should be a saint's name or one related to a Christian mystery or virtue; the patron saint is a model of discipleship and an intercessor in heaven. God calls each of us by name; thus we should begin our day, our prayers, and our activities by invoking Father, Son, and Holy Spirit in the Sign of the Cross (C 2142-2167).

The Third Commandment:

Remember to keep holy the Lord's Day.

Genesis relates that God rested on the seventh day after the work of creation. This is seen as a pattern for human activity and rest in remembrance of our dependence upon God and of our covenant with God. Jesus himself respected the holiness of the Jewish sabbath, but he also revealed its highest meaning. After his Resurrection on the first day of the week, Christians observed Sunday as the Lord's Day; they assembled to honor Jesus and to worship God in the New Covenant of love. In imitation of them, we gather with the parish community under the leadership of the pastor to express our unity in Christ. We obey the Lord's injunction to celebrate the Eucharist in memory of him. We are obliged to observe the Lord's Day and holy days of obligation by attending Mass. Those who deliberately miss Mass on these days commit a grave sin unless they are excused by a serious reason. The Church's law also commands us to rest from work or activities that hinder the worship owed to God and the joy and relaxation proper to the Lord's Day. Sanctifying Sundays means devoting time to relaxation, family, works of charity, and concern for the poor and needy. All should refrain from making demands on others which might prevent proper observance of the Lord's Day. We should consciously give witness to the world of our belief in Christ by our Sunday rest and worship (C 2168-2195).

A student was asked to list the Ten Commandments in any order. He wrote: 3,

6, 1, 8, 4, 5, 9, 2, 10, 7! We've done better! We have reflected on the first three commandments, which direct our relationship with God. In the next chapter we will turn to the last seven, which govern relationships with others.

Questions for Discussion or Reflection

Explain in your own words each of the following: moral law, natural law, justification, grace, merit, holiness.

Modern people are much influenced by the media, especially television and movies. Which movies have you seen that might encourage people to keep the first three commandments? Which movies have you seen that might influence people not to keep these commandments?

Activities

Reflect on the first three commandments. Be conscious of observing these commandments as you spend some time in adoration and prayer.

Chapter Eleven

GOD'S COMMANDMENTS
AND LOVE OF NEIGHBOR

Edrea explained to a class of preschoolers how Jesus entered Jerusalem on Palm Sunday. Afterward, a mother reported to Edrea that she asked her son what he had learned. "I learned," he replied, "that when I throw my clothes on the floor I'm praising Jesus."

Next class Edrea had to add that obedience to parents praises Jesus! The *Catechism* continues its explanation of the commandments by teaching that the last seven are summed up in the law of love of neighbor. Since love of neighbor is intimately related to love of God, obeying these commandments gives praise to God.

The Fourth Commandment:
Honor your father and your mother.

This commandment shows that we owe our parents, after God, honor and respect. It is addressed to children because the bond of children to parents is universal, but it also covers duties to family, relatives, and authorities. The commandment includes the responsibilities of authorities to those governed. It promises material benefits as well as spiritual blessings, for its observance brings peace and prosperity to society (C 2196-2200).

The family was established when God created man and woman. Each family is formed by matrimonial consent and is ordered to the good of the spouses and to the procreation and education of children. The Christian family is a communion of persons, a sign of the unity of Father, Son, and Holy Spirit. It is a domestic church—a community of faith, hope, and charity (C 2201-2206).

The family is the original cell of society and is essential to society's well-being. In the family we learn moral values and concern for others, especially the needy. Civil authority should support and protect the family, ensuring its right to exist and nurture children in peace, religious freedom, and dignity. In a caring society, the family flourishes and shows that all relationships are personal and familial under God the Father (C 2207-2213).

The duties of children include respect and gratitude for the gift of life. As long as children live in their parents' home, they owe obedience to their parents. Children also owe obedience to teachers and others to whom they have been entrusted. Adult children should continue to respect their parents, offering them care and support in old age. Family members should treat one another with love. Christians should show gratitude to those who brought them the faith (C 2214-2220).

Parental duties implied by the fourth commandment include the moral education and spiritual formation of children. Parents are the first teachers of their children and should create a home where they can learn Christ's Gospel, Christian virtues, and responsibilities toward others. Parents should provide for the spiritual and physical needs of children. Parents have a right to choose a school corresponding to their own religious convictions. They may advise adult children, but must respect their children's right to choose a spouse and a profession. They should realize that our first vocation is to follow Jesus, and they should welcome God's call to any child to serve Christ in the priesthood or religious life (C 2221-2233).

The fourth commandment addresses the duties and rights of civil authorities and citizens. Those in authority must follow the norms of natural law, respect the dignity of citizens, and serve the common good. Citizens should regard legitimate authorities as God's representatives and should promote the well-being of society. They are obliged to pay taxes, vote, and defend their country. However, they must disobey any directive contrary to God's law. Armed resistance to oppression is sometimes legitimate, but only under very limited conditions. Every society is inspired by a vision of humanity and its destiny, and the Church encourages political authorities to form a vision based on God's revealed truth. While the Church is not linked to any political community, it encourages political freedom and must pass moral judgment on issues involving fundamental human rights and the salvation of souls (C 2234-2257).

The Fifth Commandment:
You shall not kill.

Human life is sacred because it comes from God. The Old Testament forbids the killing of innocent people, and Jesus condemned hatred and vengeance, asking us to love even our enemies. Because we have a right to life, we may defend ourselves against an unjust aggressor to the point of causing death if necessary. Civil authority may defend citizens and restrain criminals by punishment or even in cases of extreme gravity, by the death penalty. The primary effect of punishment is to rectify the disorder caused by crime. Punishment should also preserve public safety and correct the offender insofar as possible. Authority should use bloodless means wherever feasible to maintain order (C 2258-2267).

This commandment forbids direct and intentional killing of the innocent as well as actions or neglect that could cause indirect killing of others. Human life must be respected from the first moment of conception. Therefore, direct abortions are gravely sinful; to emphasize the evil, the Church has attached the canonical penalty of excommunication to those who procure an abortion. Prenatal treatment is legitimate, but diagnoses directed toward abortion are forbidden, as are nontherapeutic genetic manipulations. Euthanasia, the direct killing of sick, handicapped, or dying persons, is morally unacceptable. However, medical procedures which are disproportionate to the expected outcome may be refused, and painkillers may be used to alleviate suffering, even at the risk of shortening life. Suicide is wrong because it destroys life that comes from God, because it is contrary to love of self and others, and because it can give scandal. Grave psychological disturbances, fear, and suffering can diminish the responsibility of those committing suicide, and we must commend to God's mercy those who take their own lives (C 2268-2283).

The fifth commandment promotes respect for human dignity. It forbids scandal, which is an attitude or behavior leading another to do evil. Scandal can be caused by individuals, laws or institutions, fashions or opinion. It is gravely sinful if it leads another into a serious offense. The fifth commandment mandates care of one's health because life and health are God's gifts; thus the commandment prohibits the abuse of food, alcohol, tobacco, drugs, and medicine. Those who seriously endanger others by misuse of drugs and alcohol commit a grave offense. Scientific research can benefit the common good and promote public health, but it must comply with natural law and human dignity. Organ transplants are morally acceptable only with the consent of donors or those who can legitimately speak for them. Kidnapping and hostage taking, terrorism, and torture are morally wrong. Amputations and surgery without therapeutic reasons, mutilations, and sterilizations performed on innocent persons are contrary to moral law. The dying should be given the care necessary to live their last moments in dignity and peace. The bodies of the dead must be treated with respect. Autopsies are permitted for legitimate reasons. Cremation is allowed unless it is intended as a demonstration against belief in resurrection (C 2284-2301).

Christ forbade the sins of revenge, hatred, and unjust anger. Jesus came to bring peace to the world, and respect for human life calls for peacemaking through works of justice and love. All should strive for the elimination of war. Because of human sinfulness, however, the danger of war persists, and governments have the right of legitimate self-defense. Such defense by military force is subject to rigorous conditions traditionally expressed in the "just war" doctrine. Public authorities may impose on citizens those obligations necessary for national defense. Those who serve honorably in the armed forces promote the common good and the cause of peace. Those who refuse to bear arms for reasons of conscience must be allowed to serve their country in some other way. When armed conflict breaks out, the moral law must still be respected. Actions such as the deliberate killing of non-combatants, genocide, and the indiscriminate destruction of whole cities are morally evil. The arms race does not ensure peace; instead, it brings the potential for much evil. The production and sale of weapons must be governed by public authority. Conditions such as injustice and inequality which threaten peace must be overcome (C 2302-2330).

The Sixth Commandment:
You shall not commit adultery.

God, who is love, created man and woman in the divine image, giving them the vocation to love. Sexuality affects every aspect of human life, especially the capacity to love, procreate, and form bonds of communion. Affirming one's sexual identity means acknowledging the differences and complementarity of man and woman. The union of man and woman in marriage imitates the Creator's generosity and fecundity (quality of giving life), and Jesus came to restore creation to the purity intended by God (C 2331-2336).

Chastity is the integration of sexuality within one's self and in the gift of self to others. We must learn to master our passions by self-knowledge, asceticism (self-denial, spiritual discipline), obedience to the commandments, exercise of the moral virtues, and prayer. Chastity, an aspect of the cardinal virtue of temperance, is the work of a lifetime, involving gradual growth, personal and cultural effort, and above all the grace of God. Chastity as a gift of self to others flows from charity and is expressed in friendship. All believers are called to chastity suited to their vocation: conjugal chastity for the married and continence for the unmarried. Sins against chastity include lust, masturbation, fornication, pornography, prostitution, and rape. Homosexual tendencies are not in themselves sinful, but homosexual acts are contrary to natural law (C 2337-2359).

Sexuality is ordered toward married love through which husband and wife give themselves to each other for life. The joy and pleasure of sexual acts between married couples are intended by God. The union of husband and wife achieves the twofold purpose of marriage: the good of the spouses and the transmission of life. Marriage was established by God as a partnership with obligations of fidelity and fecundity. The spouses are called to imitate the faithfulness of God, remaining true to the marriage bond which is unique and indissoluble. They must also follow God's plan that each and every marriage act be open to the transmission of life. Spouses may space the births of their children, but their motives ought to be right and their methods must be natural, respecting God's design and avoiding artificial means of contraception. Children are a sign of God's blessing, and couples who are sterile often suffer greatly. Research aimed at reducing sterility by moral means is encouraged. Techniques that require the introduction of third parties by the use of donated sperm or ova are gravely immoral. Techniques which involve only the married couple but disassociate the sexual act from the procreative act are morally unacceptable. No one has an absolute right to children, for they are not property. Where conception remains impossible after legitimate medical procedures have been exhausted, the couple should unite themselves to the Lord's cross and may consider the possibility of adoption (C 2360-2379).

Adultery—sexual relations between two people, of whom at least one is married to another—is a sin against the dignity of marriage. This sin violates the laws of both the Old and New Testaments, is an injustice against the other spouse and the family, and introduces disorder into society. Divorce is forbidden by Jesus, who clarified God's intention that marriage be indissoluble. Civil divorce is permissible, however, when it is the only way to protect legal rights or the care of children. Divorce situations vary widely. A spouse who callously abandons the family and seeks divorce sins grievously against God's law; contracting a new civil marriage adds the sin of public adultery. A spouse who has honored the marriage commitment but who is abandoned does not sin if obliged to seek a divorce for legal protection. A distinction must also be made between divorces after valid marriages and divorces after ceremonies that did not result in a true marriage before God (C 1629). Other sins against marriage include polygamy, incest, sexual abuse, free unions ("living together"), and trial marriages (C 2380-2400).

The Seventh Commandment:
You shall not steal.

This commandment forbids unjustly taking or harming the property of others. It mandates the administration of material possessions with justice and charity. At creation God entrusted the world to the whole human race. For good reasons resources have been divided and people have a right to private property. All holdings, however, should be directed to the common good, as well as to the benefit of the owner (C 2401-2406).

The seventh commandment forbids theft, the taking of property against the reasonable will of its owner. A grave need for food, clothing, or shelter can allow someone to take and use another's property. Unjust assaults upon another's property are forbidden, including retention of wages, fraud, price fixing, corruption, shoddy work, tax evasion, forgery, false expense accounts, and vandalism. Promises and contracts must be honored. Commutative justice, which regulates exchanges between individuals, demands restitution of goods taken from another. Bets and games of chance are acceptable as long as they do not involve cheating or taking what is needed for necessities. Any enslavement or misuse of human beings for profit is immoral. Material resources, plants, and animals are intended by God for human use, always with concern for the common good and for future generations. While animals may be domesticated or used for food and clothing, they should not be treated cruelly (C 2407-2418).

The Church's social doctrine brings moral judgments to economic issues involving fundamental human rights or the salvation of souls. Based on Christ's teaching and the guidance of the Holy Spirit, this doctrine provides principles, criteria for judgment, and guidelines for action. It deems unacceptable any system that makes profit the sole norm for economic activity. It rejects the atheistic ideologies associated with the communism and socialism. It also rejects exclusive reliance upon the marketplace in capitalism. Economic activity must be directed to the common good. Work is ordained by God and can be a means of sanctification. All should be able to draw a livelihood from their work. Conflicts arising from economic interplay should be resolved peacefully, through negotiation if possible. Strikes may be permitted if they are necessary to obtain a proportionate benefit. The state should guarantee freedom, private property, a stable currency, and public services. People should have access to employment and to a fair wage, and they have the obligation to pay social security contributions. On the international level, there must be an effort to reduce the inequities between wealthy and poor nations. Unjust business and financial institutions must be reformed to promote fair relationships among nations. The lay faithful are especially called to bring an awareness of God, justice, charity, and solidarity to the marketplace (C 2419-2442).

God calls us to care for the poor, and love for the poor is part of the Church's tradition. We aid the poor through the spiritual and corporal works of mercy. The former include instructing, advising, consoling, comforting, forgiving, and bearing wrongs patiently. The latter include feeding the hungry, sheltering the homeless, clothing the naked, visiting the sick and imprisoned, and burying the dead. Almsgiving is a special work of charity and justice. Christ showed compassion for those in misery, and the Church, by a preferential love for the poor, works to bring relief and justice to those in need (C 2443-2463).

The Eighth Commandment:
You shall not bear false witness against your neighbor.

This commandment prohibits misrepresenting the truth; it bids us to witness to God, whom Scripture proclaims as the source of truth. We are obliged to seek truth and to express it with sincerity, for mutual confidence among human beings is necessary for social relationships. Above all, we must be witnesses in word and deed for Christ, who is Truth. For him the martyrs gave even their lives (C 2464-2474).

The eighth commandment forbids false statements, false witness in court, and perjury (lying under oath). Respect for truth and the reputation of others forbids rash judgment (assigning moral fault to another without sufficient reason), detraction (disclosing another's faults without good reason), and calumny (telling lies about another). Honesty prohibits flattery, adulation, boasting, harmful irony, and lying. Lying means speaking falsehood with the intention of deceiving those who have a right to the truth. Lies become mortally sinful when they do grave harm. Reparation must be made for offenses against justice and truth to the extent that this is possible. In some cases, people who seek information may have no right to it; here charity and respect for truth may require silence or discreet language. Priests may never violate the seal of confession. Professional secrets must be kept, except when to do so would cause grave harm. All should respect the private lives of others. Those in the media must divulge information with concern for the common good and with respect for the rights of individuals. Civil authorities should guard against abuses in the media and must not manipulate the media for selfish purposes (C 2475-2499).

Truth, which is conformity between reality and our expression of it, is beautiful in itself. God's truth is revealed in created things and in the words of Scripture. Our relationship with God's truth and beauty can be expressed in art, especially sacred art, which evokes the mystery and grandeur of God. Genuine art draws us to adoration, prayer, and love of God; religious art should be in conformity with the truth and beauty of faith (C 2500-2513).

The Ninth Commandment:
You shall not covet your neighbor's wife.

This commandment warns against lust and carnal concupiscence, which is desire of the sensitive appetite for something contrary to human reason. It brands as immoral any intention or desire to commit acts forbidden by the sixth commandment. It directs us to observe the sixth beatitude, striving for that purity of heart which promises we shall see God in heaven and which allows us to see others as God does. Helped by God's grace, we are called to struggle for purity through chastity, pure intentions, and prayer. Purity of heart requires modesty expressed in patience, decency, and discretion. It resists immoral excesses in advertising and the media, seeks to teach modesty to the young, strives to promote a moral social climate, and conquers permissiveness with the Good News of Christ (C 2514-2533).

The Tenth Commandment:
You shall not covet your neighbor's goods.

This commandment forbids craving another's possessions and prohibits any desire to commit actions forbidden by the seventh commandment. We desire pleasant things, and desires are good unless they exceed the bounds of reason and drive us to covet unjustly what belongs to others. Forbidden by this commandment are greed, avarice, and the intention of depriving another of temporal goods. Not forbidden is the desire to acquire things by just means. Envy—sadness at the sight of another's possessions and the immoderate desire to acquire them—is a capital sin, mortal if it wishes great harm to another. We must battle envy with love, humility, and attentiveness to God, who alone can satisfy our needs. Jesus teaches us to choose him over any other good, so we must avoid being seduced by riches. Our great hope must be to see God in heaven. Desire for this true happiness keeps us from excessive attachment to material possessions and frees us for perfect union with God (C 2534-2557).

The last seven commandments direct us to a grace-filled relationship with others and to a proper use of the things of this world. Keeping them gives glory to God and guides us to the joy of seeing God face to face in heaven.

Questions for Discussion or Reflection

Some people question God's existence because of the presence of evil in our world. How much of this evil is due to human sinfulness? What would the world be like if, beginning tomorrow, all people began to keep the Ten Commandments?

Activities

If you do not know the Ten Commandments by heart, memorize them. Pray about each of them in turn, asking God to help you obey them. Pray that humanity may be more obedient to the commandments.

Part Four

Christian Prayer

Chapter Twelve

PRAYER

A dad, teaching his little daughter the Sign of the Cross, gave a simple test. He began, "In the name of the..." and the child replied, "Father." "And of the..." "Son." "And of the..." "Holy Spirit." Then he said, "A..." and she answered "B-C-D...."

The _Catechism_ closes its explanation of Catholicism by teaching the "ABC's" of prayer, not from A to Z, but from Alleluia to Amen!

What Is Prayer?

The _Catechism_ teaches us to believe in God, to celebrate God's love, to live by God's commandments, and to pray. Prayer is communication with God, who gives us both the desire and the ability to pray. Christian prayer is a covenant relationship with God brought about through Christ and the Holy Spirit; it is a communion of our hearts with the Trinity. Prayer is Christian insofar as it unites us with Jesus and extends throughout his Church (C 2558-2565).

Prayer in the Old Testament

By creating us, God has called us to prayer. The Book of Genesis relates that God spoke to the first human beings. Even after they sinned, God called out to people in every age. God evoked a special response of faith from Abraham and formed a covenant with him. Centuries later, this covenant was renewed when God spoke to Moses from the burning bush and then commissioned him to lead the Chosen People out of slavery. Moses spoke with God "face to face," interceding with God for others, helping his people to know the Lord as a God of love, justice, and faithfulness. Leaders like Samuel, David, and Elijah taught the Israelites to pray. The Jerusalem Temple became a focal point of worship. The Psalms developed into the prayer masterpiece of the Old Covenant. Powerful expressions of human emotions, their promises fulfilled in Christ, the Psalms still stand as patterns for prayer (C 2566-2597).

Prayer in the New Testament

Prayer finds its perfection in Jesus. From his mother he learned to pray in the manner of his Jewish ancestors. But as he demonstrated in the Temple at the age of twelve, he also prayed as the unique Son of God. He prayed before decisive moments in his life, in solitude, with others, and for others. His prayers in passages like Matthew 11:25-27, John 11:41-42, and those giving his last words from the cross demonstrate his loving union with the Father and his submission to God's will. His life of prayer unites humanity to God forever. He teaches us how to pray with hearts converted to God, with faith and filial boldness, with openness to God's will, with attentiveness, perseverance, patience, and humility. Jesus invites us to pray in his name, and he sends the Holy Spirit to guide us in prayer. He hears our prayers when we address them to him. His mother, in her *Fiat* ("Let it be done...") and *Magnificat,* is a model of prayerful obedience and self-offering for the Church (Luke 1:38,46-55; C 2598-2622).

Prayer in the Church

The Holy Spirit, who descended upon the first Christians on Pentecost as they gathered in prayer, forms the Church in its life of prayer. In the Acts of the Apostles 2:42, we find a pattern for the Church's prayer—founded on the apostles' teaching, expressed in works of love, and strengthened in the Eucharist. *Normative forms of prayer* for the Church are found in the Scriptures. In prayers of *blessing and adoration*, God blesses us in Christ with the grace of the Spirit, and we bless God, adoring God as Creator, Redeemer, and Spirit of Love. *Petition* expresses our dependence on God and asks God for forgiveness, for the coming of God's kingdom, and for other spiritual and material needs. Prayer of *intercession* imitates the prayer of Jesus for others. *Thanksgiving*, expressed especially in the Eucharist, communicates our gratitude to God for every good gift. *Praise* recognizes that God *is* God, declaring our joyful wonder at God's goodness and greatness. All these forms of prayer are contained and expressed in the Eucharist (C 2623-2649).

The Tradition of Prayer

The Holy Spirit, through sacred Tradition, teaches the Church how to pray. The sources of prayer are Scripture; liturgy; the theological virtues of faith, hope, and love; and the ordinary events of daily life (C 2650-2662).

Instructed by the Spirit, we pray to the *Father* through Jesus. We pray to *Jesus*; his name alone is a powerful prayer. *Jesus* means "God saves," and the repetition of Jesus' name has long been a traditional form of prayer, especially in the invocation "Lord Jesus Christ, Son of God, have mercy on us sinners." We pray to the *Holy Spirit*, by whose grace all prayer is inspired. We pray in communion with Mary, praising God for the graces bestowed upon Mary and asking for her prayers. The most common form of Marian prayer is the Hail Mary. Other prayers such as the rosary, litanies, and hymns honor Mary and seek her assistance (C 2663-2682).

The saints are models of prayer who intercede for us and offer many forms of prayer and schools of spirituality to guide us. The Christian family is the "domestic church" where all should first learn to pray. Other important teachers of prayer are ordained ministers, religious, catechists, prayer groups, and spiritual directors. The most appropriate places for prayer are churches, prayer corners in the home, monasteries, and places of pilgrimage (C 2683-2696).

The Life of Prayer

To remain mindful of God, we must set aside regular time for prayer. The Tradition of the Church proposes prayer at morning and evening, at mealtimes, in the Liturgy of the Hours, on Sundays, and throughout the liturgical year. We should also be aware of the three major expressions of prayer. *Vocal prayer* allows us to declare our interior feelings externally through words in imitation of Jesus, who taught his disciples the Our Father. *Meditation* is systematic reflection on the sacred truths of faith found in Scripture, the liturgy, spiritual writings, creation, and events of history. We incorporate these truths into the "book of life" by applying them to our own situation. We use thought, imagination, emotion, and desire to unite ourselves more closely to the heart, mind, and will of Jesus. *Contemplation* is dwelling in God's presence, focusing our attention on the Lord. We give God our time and ourselves and seek union with Father, Son, and Holy Spirit through their grace and love. We put our faith in God, unite our will to God's, and become one with the prayer of Jesus (C 2697-2724).

Prayer is sometimes a battle against our own weaknesses and the devil's temptations. We must overcome erroneous notions that reduce prayer to mere psychological activity or to anything less than a gift of God's grace. We must reject worldly attitudes like those that exalt rationalism and sensuality. We must confront discouragement, which haunts us with the notion that it does no good to pray. Prayer requires constant effort to overcome the difficulties of distractions and dryness. We do this by centering our attention on Christ through faith, conversion, and vigilance. Prayer is challenged by temptations, such as lack of faith and *acedia*, depression flowing from laxity and lukewarmness. Prayer can be undermined by feelings that our petitions are not heard; if this happens, we must examine our attitudes and motives and learn to pray as Jesus did, seeking only what pleases the Father. Jesus teaches us to focus on the Giver rather than on the gifts and to dispose ourselves to receive the Holy Spirit, who contains all good gifts. When we persevere in love, we discover that it is always possible to pray and that prayer is absolutely necessary, for prayer and Christian life are inseparable (C 2725-2745).

At the hour of his greatest struggle, the hour of his paschal mystery, Jesus offered his "priestly" prayer (John 17). This prayer sums up the great mysteries of creation and salvation. It fulfills the petitions of the prayer that Jesus taught us— the Our Father—to which we now turn (C 2746-2758).

The Lord's Prayer

When Jesus' disciples asked him how to pray, he taught them the Lord's Prayer, also called the Our Father. The version of this prayer recited at Mass is based on the text of Matthew 6:9-13. The Lord's Prayer summarizes the Gospel and is the most perfect of prayers. It is addressed to the Father, taught us by the Lord Jesus, and inspired by the Spirit. It is an integral part of the Liturgy of the Hours and the sacraments of initiation. It sums up the prayers of the Mass and directs us to the ultimate reality of Christ's coming (C 2759-2776).

"Our Father, who art in heaven"

We are able to call God "Father" only because Jesus revealed God as Father and because the Holy Spirit enables us to address God with this title. When we "dare" to call God "Father," we must realize that God transcends all limitations, including those associated with human expressions of paternity or maternity. We can call God "Father" because by Baptism we are reborn to new life, adopted as God's children, and incorporated into the Body of Christ. Praying to God as Father should give us two fundamental dispositions: a desire to be more like God by responding to God's grace, and a humble, trusting heart (C 2777-2785).

In calling God *our* Father, we do not mean that God belongs to us, but that a new relationship to God has been given us by Jesus in his new covenant. Through Baptism we are adopted as God's children. Because the Holy Trinity is consubstantial and indivisible, we adore the Father together with the Son and the Holy Spirit. When we say *our* instead of *my*, we acknowledge one God who is Father of the entire community of believers, the Church. In spite of divisions, Christians pray to one Father. Consequently, we must exclude no one from our prayer and should remember all those for whom Christ died (C 2786-2793).

We pray "Our Father, *who art in heaven*." Heaven does not refer to a place apart, but to God's limitless majesty and God's universal presence, even in the hearts of the just. Heaven is the Father's house, our true homeland, where we belong and where, by the grace of Christ, we are destined to dwell (C 2794-2802).

After addressing God as Father, we make seven petitions. The first three focus on God's glory, the last four on our needs (C 2803-2806).

"Hallowed be thy name"

These words do not mean that we can make God's name holy, but that we are to recognize God's name as holy. These words can be taken as an expression of praise, but they are intended by Jesus as a petition. We ask that God's name be glorified, as it is when we believe in God and accomplish God's work. In the covenant that God established with the Chosen People through leaders like Abraham and Moses, the holiness of God's name was gradually revealed. But many of God's people were unfaithful to the covenant and profaned God's name. Finally, Jesus revealed and glorified God's name perfectly. When we are baptized into Christ, we are called to imitate him by glorifying God's name in our life and prayer so that all may reverence God's name (C 2807-2815).

"Thy kingdom come"

The kingdom is God's loving rule, established in Christ and destined to be perfected at the end of time. In this petition, we long for the Final Coming of God's kingdom through Christ's return. We also commit ourselves to help bring about God's kingdom on earth by defeating sin and working for justice and peace. God's kingdom is not the same as earthly progress, but real commitment to the kingdom will strengthen our efforts to make this world better (C 2816-2821).

"Thy will be done on earth as it is in heaven"

God's will is that all should know the truth and be saved and that we should love one another as Christ loves us (1 Timothy 2:3-4; John 13:34). Christ obeyed God's will perfectly, and we ask God to unite our will to Christ's so that, with the Holy Spirit's help, we might do what God wants. God's will is already done in heaven, and this petition unites us to Mary and the saints, who have been obedient to God's will (C 2822-2827).

"Give us this day our daily bread"

God is the giver of every good gift, and therefore we ask God our Father for our "bread"—our material and spiritual needs. To be freed from needless worry, we entrust to God our own cares and those of the whole world. Thus we are drawn to show practical concern for the poor, to share our material and spiritual blessings, and to bring justice to personal, social, economic, and international relationships. For ourselves and for others, we seek the bread of God's Word and the Bread of Life, the Eucharist. We seek our "daily" bread, trusting that God will provide what we need every day of our lives to bring us to the everlasting day of heaven (C 2828-2837).

"And forgive us our trespasses as we forgive those who trespass against us"

Here we ask God's pardon for our sins, acknowledging that God's forgiveness can touch us only if we open ourselves to it by forgiving others, even our enemies. Real forgiveness is possible only with the help of the Holy Spirit and with the realization that love is stronger than sin. We see this in the example of Christ and the witness of the martyrs, who conquered evil by compassion (C 2838-2845).

"And lead us not into temptation"

This traditional English translation of the original New Testament Greek text seems to imply that God could lead us into temptation and thus into sin. But God cannot possibly tempt us to sin. A more accurate translation might be "Do not allow us to enter into temptation" or "Do not let us surrender to temptation." We distinguish between temptation and trials, which can actually strengthen us. We realize that being tempted is not the same as giving in to temptation. With the Holy Spirit's help, we discern that temptation is a lie which promises good though it brings evil. We seek strength from God to overcome temptation. We commit ourselves to vigilance in company with Christ. We pray for the grace of final perseverance in the last temptations of this life (C 2846-2849).

"But deliver us from evil"

In union with Christ and the Church, we ask to be delivered from the Evil One, Satan (John 17:15). Sin entered the world because human beings were deceived by the devil's temptations. Christ defeated Satan, but Satan continues to wage war against the Church. In imitation of Mary, who never sinned, we seek to withstand Satan's wiles, and we ask God to deliver humanity from every evil (C 2850-2854).

At the Eucharist we add a final prayer of praise: "For the kingdom, the power, and the glory are yours, now and for ever." These words, not found in the New Testament, were used in the liturgy of the early Church as a response to the Lord's Prayer. With these words we praise God and then add our "Amen," "So be it." We affirm what Jesus proclaims in his prayer (C 2855-2865).

In Part Four of the Catechism, the Church teaches the "ABC's" of prayer and joins us to the prayer of Jesus. What better way to respond—and close—this catechism handbook than with the traditional words of praise and assent: Alleluia! Amen!

Questions for Discussion or Reflection

Do you have a special place and time for prayer? What has been your most moving experience of vocal prayer? meditation? contemplative prayer?

Do you ever feel that your prayers are not being heard? What remedies does the *Catechism* suggest for this problem?

What part of the *Catechism's* explanation of the Lord's Prayer did you find most helpful? Why?

Activities

Find a quiet place. Picture Jesus at your side, helping you to pray. Become aware of the presence of the Holy Spirit within you, enabling you to call God "Father." Then, slowly and reverently, pray the Lord's Prayer.

EPILOGUE

In Cape Girardeau, Missouri, several years ago, a homecoming parade occurred on Halloween. Parade participants threw candy from the floats to children watching along the route. The children stashed their candy, and then went trick or treating later that evening for a second helping of goodies. Meghan, age five, attended the parade, then set out with her father, Frank, to trick or treat. Her mother, Gail, stayed home to hand out candy to the ghosts and goblins who rang the doorbell. The numbers exceeded her expectations, and she ran out of candy. Wondering what to do, she noticed a bag of homecoming candy and decided she'd just have to use it and explain to Meghan later. When Meghan returned home, Gail told her what she'd done and apologized. "That's all right," said Meghan, "because those children would be disappointed if they didn't get candy." "I'm raising a little saint," thought Gail. She hugged her daughter and exclaimed, "Meghan, that's wonderful! I'm really proud that you didn't get upset because I gave away your candy." "Oh," said Meghan, "that wasn't my candy. It was my friend Sarah's. I hid mine upstairs under my bed."

Put away the halo for now! Meghan isn't quite ready for canonization. And neither are most of us. Holiness is the work of a lifetime. The *Catechism of the Catholic Church* is the manual given us by our Catholic family to guide us on the pathway to holiness and to eternal life. So many true saints have trod this path already. They have followed the guidelines which have been set out for us in the Scriptures and in the *Catechism*. They pray for us and serve as models for our imitation.

> Therefore, since we are surrounded by so great a cloud of witnesses, let us also lay aside every weight and the sin that clings so closely, and let us run with perseverance the race that is set before us, looking to Jesus the pioneer and perfecter of our faith, who...has taken his seat at the right hand of the throne of God.
>
> *Hebrews 12:1-2*

INDEX

Abortion 89
Agnosticism 83
Amen, meaning 45
Angels 19
   guardian angels 19
Animals 92
Annulments 66
Annunciation 24
Anointing of the Sick 63
Apostles 26, 37, 40
Atheism 83

Baltimore Catechism 3
Baptism 52
Beatitudes 71
Belief in God 15
Bible
   books of 11
Bishops 40, 64
   college of 40

Catechesis 5
Catechism
   definition 3
Catechism of the Catholic Church
   need and value 2
   Prologue 5
   using the Catechism 4
Catholic Church 33
Charisms 80
Charity 74, 83
Chastity 90
Christ 23
Christian, meaning 39
Church
   and salvation 37
   apostolic 37

as mystery 34
as sacrament 34
Body of Christ 35, 42
catholic 36
hierarchical constitution 40
holy 36
meaning 34
membership 37
mother and teacher 81
one 36
origin, foundation, mission 34
people of God 35
Church building 52
Commandments
   First 82
   Second 84
   Third 84
   Fourth 87
   Fifth 88
   Sixth 90
   Seventh 91
   Eighth 93
   Ninth 93
   Tenth 94
Common good 76
Communion of Saints 42
Community 75
Concupiscence 54
Confession 61
Confirmation 54
Conscience 73
Consecrated life 42
Consecrated virginity 65
Covenant 9
Creation 19
Creeds 12, 15
   Apostles' Creed 15
   Nicene Creed 15
Cremation 89

Deacons 64
Death 44
Deposit of faith 3, 10
Devil 20
Dogmas 10

Easter 51
Economy 16, 50
Eucharist 56
Euthanasia 89
Evangelical counsels 80
Evil 18
    moral 18
    physical 18

Faith 12, 74, 83
Family 87, 99
Forgiveness of sins 43
Freedom 72
Funerals 67

God 16
    belief in 16
    Creator 17
    Father 17, 100
    Holy Spirit 31
    Providence 18
    Son 23
Grace 80
    actual 80
    of state 81
    sacramental 80
    sanctifying 80

Heaven 44
Hell 45
Holiness 81
Holy Communion 57
Holy Orders 64
Holy Spirit 31
    and the Church 33

fruits 74
gifts 74
mission 31
Hope 74, 83
Humanity
    in God's image 19, 71, 75

Incarnation 24
Indulgences 62
Infallibility 40, 81

Jesus Christ 23
    Ascension 28
    "brothers and sisters" 25
    Christ, meaning 23
    crucifixion and death 27
    descent into hell 28
    God and human 24
    infancy and hidden life 25
    Jesus, meaning 23
    Judge 29
    Lord 24, 28
    mediator 27
    Messiah 23
    public life 26
    redemption 27
    Resurrection 28
    Son of God 23
John the Baptist 25, 26
Joseph
    husband of Mary 25
Judgment
    Last 45
    particular 44
Justification 54, 80

Kingdom 101

Laity 41
    priestly, prophetic, kingly offices 41
Last days 33

Last Judgment 45
Last Supper 56
Law 79
Life everlasting 44
Liturgical year 51
Liturgy 49, 51
Liturgy of the Hours 51
Lord's Prayer 100

Magisterium 10, 81
Marriage 65, 91
Mary
  Advocate, Helper, Benefactress, and
    Mediatrix 43
  full of grace 25
  "Hail Mary" 99
  Immaculate Conception 25
  Mother of Christ 25, 43
  Mother of God 25
  Mother of the Church 43
  prayer 99
  virgin 25
  virginal conception of Jesus 32
Mass 56
Matrimony 65
Merit 81
Messiah, meaning 23
Moral Law 79
Morality, of human acts 72
Mystical Body of Christ 35

Natural family planning 91
Natural law 79
New heavens and new earth 45

Original sin 20
Our Father 100

Particular judgment 44
Paschal mystery 49, 50
Passions 72

Passover 27, 56
Penance
  sacrament of 61
Pentecost 33
Peter 26, 40
Pope 40
  vicar of Christ 40
Pope John Paul II 5
Popular Piety 67
Prayer 97
  contemplation 99
  forms of 98
  in the Church 98
  Jesus' priestly prayer 100
  meditation 99
  New Testament 98
  Old Testament 97
  vocal 99
Precepts of the Church 81
Priests 64
Purgatory 43, 45

RCIA 53
Reconciliation
  sacrament of 61
Religion 83
Resurrection of the body 44
Revealed laws 79
Revelation
  private 10
  public 10
  supernatural 9, 10
Roman Catechism 3

Sacramental economy 50
Sacramentals 66
  definition of 66
Sacraments 52
  and paschal mystery 50
  character 51, 54, 55
  definition 50
  of healing 52, 61
  of initiation 52

of service 52, 64
seven 50
Saints 43, 99
Salvation 3, 21, 23, 79
Satan 20
Scandal 89
Scripture
  and Revelation 10
  authors 11
  inspiration 11
  interpretation 11
  senses of 11
Second Vatican Council 1, 5
Sin 20, 74
  capital 75
  mortal 74
  original sin 20
  venial 75
Social justice 76
Society 75
Solidarity 19, 76
Soul 19
Subsidiarity
  principle of 75
Suffering 63
Sunday
  Lord's Day 84

Temptation 102
Ten Commandments 82
Theological virtues 74
Theology 16
Tradition
  and Revelation 10
Traditions
  customs 10
Transubstantiation 57
Trent
  Council of 3
Trinity 16
Truth 93

Viaticum 63
Vices 75
Virtues 73
  cardinal 74
  human 73
  theological 74

Works of mercy 92

ABOUT THE AUTHOR

Father Oscar Lukefahr, CM, had to be persuaded by the editors at Liguori Publications to write his first book, *"We Believe..." A Survey of the Catholic Faith*, based on a series of articles he had previously written for a national church bulletin service. With that first book completed, he agreed to do a companion workbook and then planned to "call it quits" where book writing was concerned. But with the publication of *The Catechism Handbook*, Father Lukefahr (known to friends and colleagues as Father Luke) adds a fifth title to his list of books and companion workbooks. In addition, he continues to contribute articles to a weekly Sunday bulletin service and to *Liguorian*, a monthly magazine.

After ordination as a Vincentian priest, Father Lukefahr earned Master of Arts degrees in Latin from DePaul University and in Secondary Counseling from Southeast Missouri State University. He earned his Master of Divinity degree from DeAndreis Seminary.

Energetic and articulate, Father Lukefahr is in demand as a retreat director and for parish missions throughout the United States. On some pastoral travels, especially to remote locations like Kinnear, Wyoming, he has been known to take his laptop computer and fly fishing equipment. A former competitive runner and participant in ten marathons, Father Lukefahr now usually runs about twenty-five miles a week. He lives in Perryville, Missouri, at the Vincentian retirement center, close to his office at the Catholic Home Study Service.

Workbook also available...